GENETIC ENGINEERING

FACTS ON FILE
SCIENCE SOURCEBOOKS

GENETIC ENGINEERING

SHAPING THE MATERIAL OF LIFE

ELLEN THRO

Facts On File, Inc.

AN INFOBASE HOLDINGS COMPANY

On the cover: DNA purification

GENETIC ENGINEERING: SHAPING THE MATERIAL OF LIFE

Copyright © 1993 by Ellen Thro

Facts On File, Inc.
11 Penn Plaza
New York, NY 10001

Library of Congress Cataloging-in-Publication Data

Thro, Ellen.
  Genetic engineering: shaping the material of life/Ellen Thro.
    p. cm. — (Facts on File science sourcebooks)
  Includes bibliographical references and index.
  Summary: Defines and traces the history of genetic engineering and describes its uses in medicine, agriculture, and business.
    ISBN 0-8160-2629-7
    1. Genetic engineering — History — Juvenile literature.
  (1. Genetic engineering — History.) I. Title. II. Series.
  QH442.T47   1993
  660.'65—dc20   92–17256

Facts On File books are available at special discounts when purchased in bulk quantities for businesses, associations, institutions or sales promotions. Please call our Special Sales Department in New York at 212/967-8800 or 800/322-8755

Text design by Ron Monteleone
Jacket design by Amy Gonzalez
Cover photo courtesy of National Cancer Institute

Printed in the United States of America

MP FOF 10 9 8 7 6 5 4 3

This book is printed on acid-free paper

CONTENTS

Chapter 1. From One Generation to Another 1
Early Knowledge About Inheritance 1
Gregor Mendel and the Garden Peas 2
The Microscope and the Cell 4
The Beginnings of Modern Genetics 8
Viruses and Bacteria 10
DNA and the Double Helix 10
DNA and RNA 17
The Genetic Code 18
The Beginnings of Genetic Engineering 18

Chapter 2. The Cell 21
A Eukaryotic Cell 22
Cell Cycle 25
The Cell at Work 35
Cell Maintenance and Repair 37

Chapter 3. Genetic Engineering in Agriculture 40
Genetic Engineering in Animals 40
Transgenic Animals 41
Bovine Growth Hormone and Milk Production 46
Vaccines and Diagnostics 51
Genetic Engineering in Plants 52
Genetically Engineered Plants and the Natural Environment 56

Chapter 4. Genetic Fingerprinting—DNA in the Courtroom 57
Preparing DNA Samples 57
Identifying Parents 63
Identifying Criminals 63
Is Genetic Fingerprinting Reliable? 64

Chapter 5. Medical Uses of Genetic Engineering 67
The Genetics of Disease 69
Inheritance, Disease, and Genetic Engineering 70
Gene Therapy 79

Chapter 6. Genetics and Cancer 83
  The Roles of Genes in Cancer Development 84
  Bladder Cancer 86
  Li-Fraumeni Syndrome 87
  What Do Genetic Tests Mean for Society? 88
  Gene Therapy for Cancer 89

Chapter 7. Genes in Research and Business 92
  Mapping the Genome 94
  Sequencing 97
  Other Genomes 98
  Patenting Living Things 99
  Commercial Biotechnology 102
  What Does Genetic Engineering Mean for the Future? 104

Glossary 105
Further Reading 113
Index 115

1 FROM ONE GENERATION TO ANOTHER

Red, curly hair runs in some families and black, straight hair in others. Some families include many people who live into their late nineties or beyond. Eye and hair color as well as height, longevity, and other "family traits" are inherited from parents and passed on to children in cellular material called genes. Some diseases can also be inherited or caused by changes in one's own genes or those of a parent. Inheritance is a characteristic of all living things.

What are genes? What are they made of? Where are they located? How do they work? Scientists do not yet have complete answers to these questions, but they know enough to work with the genes of many species to change or improve them. The results are becoming available in the treatment of human illness, new varieties of food crops, and as a tool for preserving animals in the wild.

What are genes? The short answer is that they are tiny chunks of information or instructions, organized into chromosomes and stored in each cell of the body. They tell the body what to do, whether it's digesting lunch or growing toenails. And they divide and (in higher animals and plants) merge with other genes during sexual reproduction.

Today's knowledge is built on a long record of research about inheritance and about the basic unit of life, the cell. Both have their roots in the scientific revolution of the 17th century.

Early Knowledge About Inheritance

People seem to have known about inheritance of physical characteristics for thousands of years. It was one of the bases of early agriculture and the domestication of animals. People developed dependable crops such as corn, wheat, and rice from wild plants. They domesticated cattle, sheep, horses, camels, and dogs from wild ancestors. And they did all of this without ever knowing anything about modern genetics.

It wasn't until the 17th century that people discovered that pollen grains were the male reproductive cells of plants. This knowledge had an explosive effect, beginning what is called modern scientific agriculture. Immediately farmers and botanists began developing new varieties of grains, fruits, and vegetables and also decorative plants. Agriculture became the growth industry of the century.

In the Netherlands, for example, tulip-growing became a major industry, which it still is today. Tulip farmers raced to develop new colors before their competitors, particularly the ultimate—a black tulip. The intrigue rivaled 20th-century espionage and was described in a famous 19th-century novel by the French author Alexandre Dumas (Père) called *The Black Tulip*.

But all the improvements in plants and animals didn't provide a scientific explanation of how inheritance worked; they didn't specify what the rules of inheritance were. Understanding the rules didn't come until the 1860s, and it all happened in a quiet European monastery.

Gregor Mendel and the Garden Peas

The first scientific investigation of inheritance came from an unlikely place—a monastery garden in what later became Czechoslovakia. There in the 19th century, a monk named Gregor Mendel bred generations of pea plants, observed the way they inherited characteristics, and founded modern genetics.

Mendel used varieties of pea plants that had seven pairs of characteristics: tall plants and short plants, flowers on the sides of stems and flowers at the tip, full pod shape and flat pod shape, green peas and yellow peas, smooth peas and wrinkled peas, green pods and yellow pods, and gray pea coatings and white pea coatings.

When Mendel bred one type of plant over several generations, he found that the characteristics—say, tall and short— showed up, or were expressed, according to a regular pattern of tall and short offspring. From his findings, he determined that plants had what he called hereditary units and that when two plants reproduce sexually, the next generation receives one unit from each parent. This is his *law of segregation* or *separation*.

[National Library of Medicine, Bethesda, MD]

Gregor Mendel made early discoveries about genetics working with pea plants in his monastery garden.

Mendel also found that some units are dominant over their opposites but didn't modify, or change, them—the *law of dominance*. These two laws have proven to be almost always true, regardless of characteristic or species. (The "almost" will be explained in the next chapter.)

The following is the pattern of reproduction Mendel found. Since each plant gets one hereditary unit (today they're called genes) from each parent, let's start with one plant that had two tall parents and one with two short ones. We will use **A** to indicate the dominant characteristic of tall plants and **a** for the recessive characteristic of short ones. (A gene from only one parent can express a dominant trait. For a recessive trait to be expressed, both parents must supply it.)

AA   aa

Because these plants have two of the same genes, they are called *homozygotes*.

When these two plants reproduce, what genes do the first-generation offspring get? (This is called the first filial, or child, generation, or F1.) Remember, they get one gene from each parent.

They get one gene for "tallness" and one for "shortness" from each parent.

	A	A
a	Aa	Aa
a	Aa	Aa

Aa Aa Aa Aa

Because their tall-short traits are mixed, they are called *heterozygotes* or *hybrids*.

What do they look like? They're all tall like the **AA**, but for a different reason. The **A** gene is dominant and the **a** gene is recessive. So when a plant contains one gene of each, the **A** is always expressed.

What about the **a** gene? It's always there. But there must be two recessive genes, such as **aa**, for the recessive trait to be expressed.

Now suppose you breed two of the F1s.

Aa Aa

The second-generation (F2) offspring include the following:

	A	a
A	AA	aA
a	Aa	aa

In other words, the second-generation plants are

AA Aa aA aa

What do they look like? Three are tall and one is short.

Mendel wrote a third law to describe the expression of several different traits at the same time. However, this *law of independent assortment* is true for some traits, but not others.

At the time when Mendel was developing his laws, great advances were being made in the other strand of modern genetics, cell science.

The Microscope and the Cell

Knowledge about the cell—the other strand of modern genetics—also began during the 17th century, with one of the great inventions of the scientific revolution: the microscope.

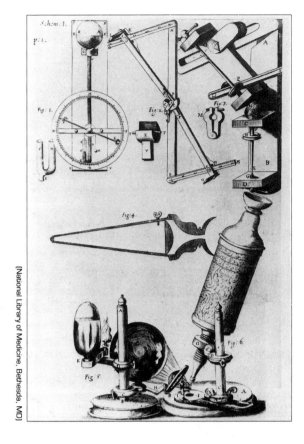

An engraving of one of Robert Hooke's microscopes from his 1667 book Micrographia. *Hooke first discovered subdivisions in plant matter and called these units cells.*

The microscope let humans see the invisible world of small structures for the first time. The Englishman Robert Hooke used a microscope to examine many plant samples and discovered that their structure was divided by rigid walls. He called the substructures cells because they reminded him of the small rooms, or cells, used by monks in monasteries.

The Dutch microscope developer Antonius van Leeuwenhoek performed similar research on animal tissues, discovering blood and sperm cells and bacteria, which he called animalcules, or small animal-shaped creatures. The name fit in with the belief that the human body contained small organs that were shaped like miniature people, called homunculuses.

Research continued throughout the 18th century, and by the early 19th, cells were found to be the structure of all living tissue. By the 1850s, scientists had observed cells dividing.

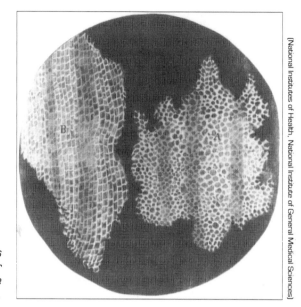

[National Institutes of Health, National Institute of General Medical Sciences]

This drawing shows what Hooke saw under his microscope—the cells in cork.

About the same time Mendel was finishing his experiments with peas, the French scientist Louis Pasteur discovered that the purpose of cell division was reproduction—living cells developing from other

[National Library of Medicine, Bethesda, MD]

A 1632 portrait of Antonius van Leeuwenhoek by Jan Verkolje. Leeuwenhoek, a Dutch microscope developer, spent most of his life making microscopes and recording what he observed under them. He was the first to observe bacteria, which he called animalcules, in various organic substances.

Louis Pasteur discovered, among other things, that the purpose of cell division was reproduction.

living cells. His finding finally put an end to an old belief in spontaneous generation—the formation of living organisms from nonliving materials. Pasteur also learned that living cells are dynamic. They use and produce energy and materials.

Throughout the 19th century, a number of scientists discovered the basic anatomy of the cell. They learned that the cells they studied were composed of a nucleus, or center, containing wormlike bodies called chromosomes. The nucleus was surrounded by a fluid called protoplasm.

One more 19th-century idea affected the study of inheritance. It was the *theory of evolution*, proposed by Charles Darwin and others, which said that species have changed and evolved over millions of years. The theory immediately raised another question: What process in the body causes evolutionary change? Since the changes occurred over generations, the question fit right in with the questions about heredity that scientists were already studying.

By the end of the century, cell scientists and those who studied inheritance realized that the source of information they sought was in the heart of a cell, its nucleus.

An 1849 portrait of Charles Darwin. In the late 1800s, Darwin developed his controversial theory of evolution.

(National Library of Medicine, Bethesda, MD)

The Beginnings of Modern Genetics

While cell science and evolution theory were advancing, what was happening in inheritance studies? Nothing! Mendel's work was quickly forgotten and not rediscovered until the year 1900. Around the turn of the century, several European scientists unknowingly duplicated Mendel's work. When they realized that he had found the same things 35 years earlier, in the best scientific tradition they quickly named Mendel the founder of modern genetics.

By the early 1900s, scientists were using Mendel's laws of segregation and dominance to develop many plants and animals and in order to understand human disease. The next area of investigation concerned what Mendel had called units, or genes. These genes make up what are now called chromosomes.

The first major discovery grew out of work on various species of insects. A cell's chromosomes normally come in identical pairs, except for the chromosomes scientists called X and Y. Females always have two X chromosomes. Males of some species have one X and one Y, but in other species males have only a single X chromosome. Scientists quickly realized that the X and Y (or lack of it) determine the individual's sex. But did these chromosomes have other functions as well?

The answer came from the first giant of 20th-century genetics, the American Thomas Hunt Morgan. In decades of research with the simple fly *Drosophila melanogaster*, Morgan and his colleagues and students discovered what the X and Y chromosomes do, and Morgan developed the theory of the gene. (*Drosophila* and humans both have the XY pairing.)

Building on Mendel's work, Morgan found that the fly's eye color is transmitted on the X chromosome—a red eye is dominant and a white eye, recessive. Morgan also found that there are two body colors, gray and yellow. Mendel's third law (independent assortment) said that eye color and body color would be transmitted independently. But Morgan found that isn't always true. Instead, they seem to be inherited together. Red eye and gray body are inherited together, and so are white eye and yellow body. Morgan called this *linkage*, and other scientists found it in different species.

Morgan decided that linkage could occur if both eye color and body color were on the same chromosome. But linkage didn't always occur. To explain this Morgan developed the theory of *crossing over* in which parts of a chromosome pair exchanged places during cell reproduction. The linked traits could then be separated.

Morgan called these different trait locations on a chromosome genes. The closer together they were, the more likely they were to stay together. As the research continued, Morgan and other scientists used the crossing-over information to draw *linkage maps*, showing

[National Institutes of Health, National Institute of General Medical Sciences]

Thomas Hunt Morgan performed much of his genetic research on a simple fly, Drosophila melanogaster, *shown here. Having only four pairs of chromosomes, rather than the 23 pairs humans have,* Drosophila *were much easier to work with.*

the locations of various genes on the chromosomes. Other scientists created linkage maps for many plant and animal species.

Other scientists discovered that portions of chromosomes could be changed by exposing them to high temperatures or to X rays. They called these changed chromosomes *mutations*. By the late 1930s, it was clear that a chromosome was a series of genes. This immediately raised three more questions.

- What are genes made of?
- What is their structure?
- How do they duplicate themselves when cells prepare to divide?

Viruses and Bacteria

The three questions about genes were answered during the middle third of the 20th century, with a lot of help from one-celled organisms called *bacteria* and even simpler ones called *viruses*. The first question was: What are genes made of?

In the 1930s and 1940s, scientists believed there were two possible answers: Genes were either proteins or nucleic acids. Many scientists favored proteins—the body's structural materials, made of amino acids. They believed the two nucleic acids, called *DNA* (deoxyribonucleic acid) and *RNA* (ribonucleic acid), were small, not very important molecules. Also, RNA was supposed to be found only in plant cells, so it wasn't considered seriously.

Then several groups of American scientists showed that both DNA and RNA were found in *all* cells. Oswald Avery and his coworkers discovered that if DNA is taken from one type of bacteria and put in a second type, the DNA of the second bacteria takes on characteristics of the first type. And the bacteria that provided the DNA were known to have inherited these characteristics.

Viruses are simpler than cells and cannot live independently. Viruses were believed to be mostly gene. In 1949 Arthur Mirsky discovered that genes were made of DNA. And in 1952 Alfred Hershey and Martha Chase found that transferring a virus's DNA to another organism infected the organisms just as the virus itself would.

DNA and the Double Helix

By the early 1950s, scientists knew that DNA is a very long molecule built from subunits called *nucleotides*. Each nucleotide, in turn, is composed of three small molecules. Two of the molecules, phosphoric acid and a sugar, are joined sugar-phosphate-sugar and so on. They serve as DNA's backbone or structural material. Each sugar molecule has attached to it one of four molecules called *bases*.

Two of the bases are *purines* called *adenine* (which is abbreviated (A) and *guanine* (G). The other two bases are *pyrimidines*, named *cytosine* (C) and *thymine* (T).

Scientists knew what the subparts were, but how the whole thing was put together was still a mystery. There was a good clue, though. The American chemist George Wells Beadle and others showed—using mutations of bread mold—that each gene controlled the production of a single enzyme (protein). In 1951 another American chemist, Linus Pauling, showed for the first time that a protein molecule is in the shape of a *helix*—similar to the spiral wire on a notebook. The next year other scientists discovered that RNA is a single helix. So they believed that DNA was probably a helix too.

The American scientist James Watson and three British scientists, Francis Crick, Maurice Wilkins, and Rosalind Franklin, took this idea and solved the DNA mystery. Doing so involved answering several more questions, such as:

- How many strands are there in the DNA helix?
- Is the backbone in the middle or on the outside?

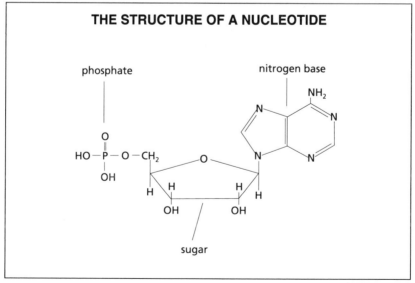

THE STRUCTURE OF A NUCLEOTIDE

Figure 1

A CHAIN OF NUCLEOTIDES

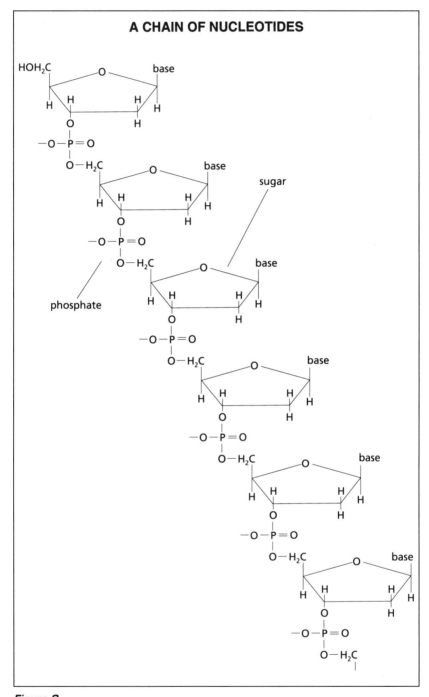

Figure 2

THE COMPONENTS OF DNA MOLECULE

sugar molecule

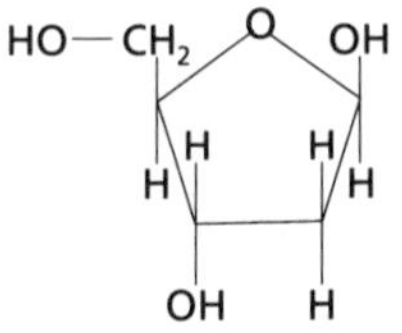

phosphate group

2-deoxyribose

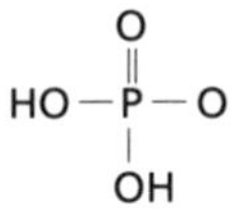

four nitrogen bases

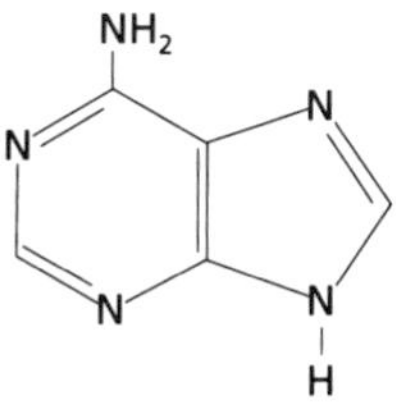

adenine 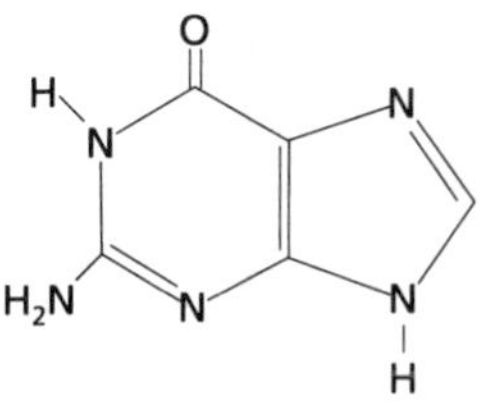   guanine 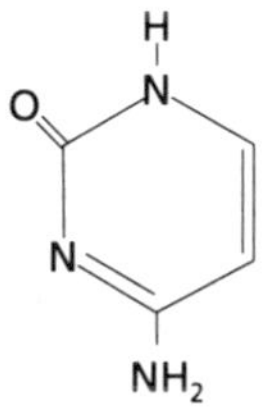   cytosine 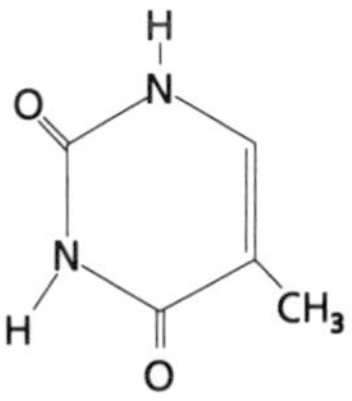   thymine

key:

O = oxygen atom
H = hydrogen atom
N = nitrogen atom
P = phosphorus atom

A carbon atom is understood to be located at the intersection of any four lines in a formula.

A single line (———) in a formula represents a single covalent bond, that is, a pair of shared electrons.

A double line (═══) in a formula represents a double covalent bond, that is, two pairs of shared electrons.

Figure 3

(Courtesy of Caltech)

Linus Pauling sits next to a model of a helix. Pauling was the first to discover that a protein molecule was helical.

- What holds the strands together?

The best clue they had to DNA's structure came from a discovery by the American Erwin Chargaff of the three characteristics of any DNA segment:

- equal numbers of purines and pyrimidines,
- as many of the purine As as the pyrimidine Ts, and
- as many purine Gs as pyrimidine Cs.

But the ratio of AT to CG was different from one species to another.

It was not clear how all this information fit together to explain DNA's stable structure. The scientists had to figure out how many strands DNA had—one, two, or three. Watson and Crick tried two and, based on the work of colleagues, decided to put each strand's backbone on the outside.

The shape would be a two-stranded or *double helix*, very much like a spiraling ladder, with the backbones serving as legs and the bases

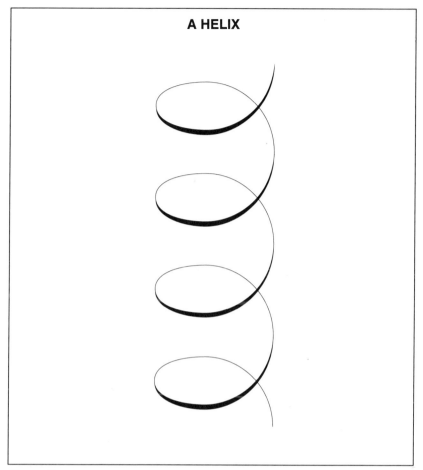

A HELIX

Figure 4

joined in the middle as rungs. But the scientists were still unsure exactly how the bases joined together. Crick and Watson tried various combinations. They thought about linking the two purines together and also the two pyrimidines, but this wouldn't work because purines and pyrimidines were different sizes. And the two purines were different, as were the two pyrimidines. All the rungs of the ladder had to be the same width, or it would buckle.

Crick and Watson then realized there was only one possible combination. A purine A always had to be linked to a pyrimidine T, and a purine G to a pyrimidine C. This way the ladder rungs would always be the same width. Hydrogen bonds connected each rung's A-T or C-G in the middle, forming what is called a *base pair*.

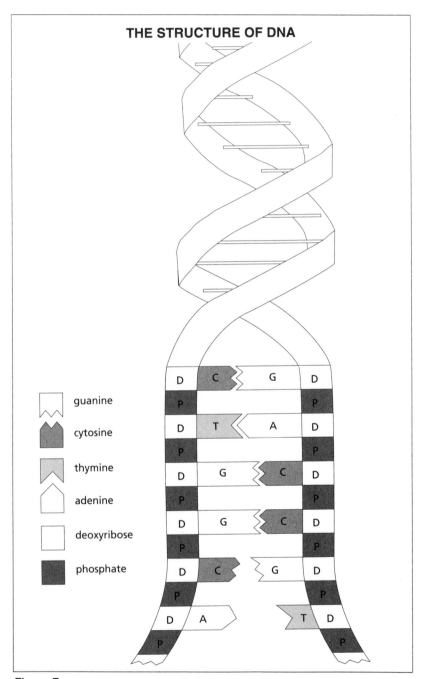

THE STRUCTURE OF DNA

Figure 5

DNA and RNA

At the same time DNA's double helix shape was being discovered, other scientists had found that the two nucleic acids, DNA and RNA, formed at the same time during cell division. Did this mean that DNA turned into RNA? And how did this relate to the fact that one gene was associated with one protein?

The answer was that cellular DNA formed RNA, which in turn formed proteins. This central belief or dogma, as Francis Crick has called it, made possible the research field of *molecular biology* and the medical and other techniques of *genetic engineering*.

It also means that DNA and RNA are very important to people in everyday life. The human body is built of proteins. Muscle is made of protein, and so are the chemicals that perform every function of every cell.

How does DNA make RNA, so RNA can make protein? To understand the question, a closer look at DNA and RNA is needed. They are both a type of nucleic acid, but they have some differences:

	DNA **(Dioxyribonucleic Acid)**	**RNA** **(Ribonucleic Acid)**
Sugar structure:	dioxyribose	ribose
Number of strands:	two	one
Pyrimidines:	thymine (T)	uracil (U)

[National Institutes of Health, National Institute of General Medical Sciences]

A strand of DNA as seen under an electron microscope.

After the structure of the two nucleic acids was discovered, there was still one big mystery. What did the structure mean?

The Genetic Code

Inside each cell in the human body is DNA inherited from one's parents. This DNA is sort of the body's instruction manual. It is a code for many of the body's characteristics. This code is not written in the 26-letter English language. It's written in just four letters—A, C, G, and T. It has 46 "chapters"—23 pairs of chromosomes, for humans. Each human has billions of copies of it—one in each cell. The genetic code is the order in which the purines and pyrimidines are arranged along a chromosome. For example, TGACCA has a different meaning from GATCAC.

The next thing scientists wanted to figure out was what the key to decoding was and how the letters related to the proteins. Proteins are made up of amino acids, and there are 20 amino acids. So scientists asked: Can one base—an A or a C, for instance—be responsible for one amino acid? The answer was no, because there are only four bases.

How about two bases per amino acid? Again no, because there are only 16 possible combinations of A, C, G, and T. But how about three bases per amino acid? This would give 64 possible combinations.

Experiments involving natural and mutated genes showed that three bases was the right answer. The first actual decoding was done in 1961 by the Americans Marshall Nirenberg and Heinrich Matthei. They mixed a batch of RNA and amino acids and observed the protein that resulted. A series of similar experiments over the next few years provided the entire genetic code.

Each group of three consecutive nucleotides is called a *triplet* or *codon*. Since there are 64 possible "words" and only 20 amino acids, some of the words are synonyms. That is, there is more than one code "word" for some amino acids. The code is written in terms of RNA. For instance, UUA is the code for leucine, but so are UUG, CUU, CUC, CUA, and CUG.

The Beginnings of Genetic Engineering

By the early 1960s, the French scientists Jacques Monod and Francois Jacob showed that genes can be turned on and off by what are called *regulator genes*. Genes that are on can direct protein production. If genes are off, they're inactive. In the early 1970s, the first successful

THE GENETIC CODE

Second base

		U		C		A		G		
First base	**U**	UUU	Phe	UCU	Ser	UAU	Tyr	UGU	Cys	U
		UUC	Phe	UCC	Ser	UAC	Tyr	UGC	Cys	C
		UUA	Leu	UCA	Ser	UAA	Stop	UGA	Stop	A
		UUG	Leu	UCG	Ser	UAG	Stop	UGG	Trp	G
	C	CUU	Leu	CCU	Pro	CAU	His	CGU	Arg	U
		CUC	Leu	CCC	Pro	CAC	His	CGC	Arg	C
		CUA	Leu	CCA	Pro	CAA	Gln	CGA	Arg	A
		CUG	Leu	CCG	Pro	CAG	Gln	CGG	Arg	G
	A	AUU	Ile	ACU	Thr	AAU	Asn	AGU	Ser	U
		AUC	Ile	ACC	Thr	AAC	Asn	AGC	Ser	C
		AUA	Ile	ACA	Thr	AAA	Lys	AGA	Arg	A
		AUG	Met (start)	ACG	Thr	AAG	Lys	AGG	Arg	G
	G	GUU	Val	GCU	Ala	GAU	Asp	GGU	Gly	U
		GUC	Val	GCC	Ala	GAC	Asp	GGC	Gly	C
		GUA	Val	GCA	Ala	GAA	Glu	GGA	Gly	A
		GUG	Val	GCG	Ala	GAG	Glu	GGG	Gly	G

(Third base)

The genetic code given above is for RNA.
The amino acid abbreviations in the code and their codons are as follows:

	Ala	alanine	GCU GCC GCA GCG
*	Arg	arginine	CGU CGC CGA CGG AGA AGG
	Asn	asparagine	AAU AAC
	Asp	aspartic acid	GAU GAC
	Cys	cysteine	UGU UGC
	Gln	glutamine	CAA CAG
	Glu	glutamic acid	GAA GAG
	Gly	glycine	GGU GGC GGA GGG
*	His	histidine	CAU CAC
*	Ile	isoleucine	AUU AUC AUA
*	Leu	leucine	UUA UUG CUU CUC CUA CUG
*	Lys	lysine	AAA AAG
*	Met	methionine	AUG (in the middle of a sequence)
*	Phe	phenylalanine	UUU UUC
	Pro	proline	CCU CCC CCA CCG
	Ser	serine	UCU UCC UCA UCG AGU AGC
*	Thr	threonine	ACU ACC ACA ACG
*	Trp	tryptophan	UGG
	Tyr	tyrosine	UAU UAC
*	Val	valine	GUU GUC GUA GUG
	Termination		UAA UAG UGA

* = essential amino acids

Figure 6

gene-altering experiment took place. And in the 1980s came the first genetically engineered plant—a disease-resistant petunia.

The DNA findings of the 1950s also provided the beginning of an answer to another question about genes: How do they duplicate themselves when cells prepare to divide? Knowledge of the cell cycle provides the basis of today's genetic engineering—and tomorrow's. The next chapter will describe the living cell and explain how DNA and RNA do their work.

2 THE CELL

A cell is a dynamic system. It is "born," lives, grows, reproduces, and dies. Each cell works like an automated factory, duplicating parts of itself. It interacts with its environment, sending and receiving signals—electrical and chemical—to act on or cause action elsewhere, and guarding against invaders or aggressively attacking other cells. A cell changes shape, moves off to another place, and sometimes links up with other cells.

A cell is the smallest independent unit of life. Experiments done several decades ago showed that ordinary physical and chemical processes of the early Earth could assemble materials into the building materials of living cells. The first organisms were single-celled. Today many species, such as bacteria, still consist of only one cell. Through millions of years, some cells combined into more complex species.

A cell is a lot like a community because it is the home of semiindependent bodies that perform specialized and individual functions as well as being working members of the cell. Some of these bodies even have their own DNA. (Lynn Margulis, a biologist now at the University of Massachusetts, Amherst, first proposed this idea in the 1960s.)

The cell's genetic material, the DNA, directs the cell's functions and also its future. A multicellular (many-celled) organism—a human, for instance—is made up of billions of cells. But human cells are organized into groups of similar cells called tissues. Different types of tissues make up organs such as the heart and systems such as the brain and nerves. Organs act as "individuals" within the body—the heart pumps blood and the stomach digests food.

This organization means that each individual cell's DNA directs how the cell interacts with others near it, within the same organ or system. And, of course, the DNA carries the genetic heritage to the next generation of cells.

There are two classes of cells. Complex cells, called *eukaryotes*, are highly organized and complex. The other class of cells—the *prokaryotes*—are less structured and are found only in some types of bacteria.

A Eukaryotic Cell

A eukaryotic cell has a *nucleus*—a central body that is clearly separated from the rest of the cell. It also has specialized bodies that perform specific tasks. Human cells are eukaryotic. So are those of animals and plants and of some bacteria.

Nucleus

The center of the cell is the nucleus. It contains *chromatin*, which is the DNA and the protein structure that supports it. Chromatin is in one of two forms. *Heterochromatin* is condensed. It contains either no genes or inactive ones, but it maintains chromatin structure. *Euchromatin* is loose. It contains active genes, the ones that control production of proteins in the cell. In human cells, chromatin is

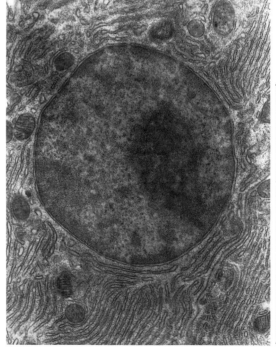

This is a cell nucleus from a eukaryotic cell. Note the double membrane surrounding it. The smaller oval bodies in the cytoplasm are mitochondria.

[National Institutes of Health, National Institute of General Medical Sciences]

organized into 23 pairs of chromosomes. In most species, including humans, the nucleus also contains round bodies called *nucleoli*. They are made of RNA and proteins. The nucleus is organized within a structure called a *nuclear matrix*.

Nuclear Membrane

The nucleus is surrounded by a double membrane filled with pores. This membrane allows cell chemicals to move between the nucleus and the surrounding *cytoplasm*.

Cytoplasm

Cytoplasm in a human cell is a fluid containing many specialized chemicals and bodies. It is supported by a *cytoskeleton* (*cyto* means cell), which is a mesh of interacting and flexible fibers. The largest of the fibers are *microtubule* protein polymers (repeating molecules). The largest skeleton fibers are called *microfilaments*. They are made of a substance that allows cells to contract or change shape, for instance, when a person flexes a muscle. The midsize *intermediary filaments* are made of fibrous proteins.

The cytoplasm mesh holds the specialized cell bodies called *organelles*. These include the cell-like *mitochondria*, which work like little engines to produce energy for cell operations.

Mitochondria

Mitochondria are semiindependent bodies in the cell. Far back in time, they may have been independent prokaryotic (simple) bacteria. When they became part of eukeryotic cells, they gave up some of their functions. For instance, the cell makes the mitochondria's structural proteins. In return, the mitochondria does some of the cell's work.

Each human cell may have as many as 100 mitochondria. The number depends on the cell's energy needs. A muscle cell, for example, needs more energy than average and so may have many more mitochondria than other types of cell.

Each mitochondrion (*mitochondria* is plural) has the simplified prokaryotic cell structure that is contained by a double membrane—a folded inner membrane and an outer membrane. It has its own DNA (known as *mtDNA*, for mitochondrial DNA) containing 37 genes. Every mtDNA is composed of about 16,569 base pairs shaped in one continuous double-strand loop. The mitochondrion produces some RNA for itself and some for the cell's ribosomes. Each mitochondrion contains between four and 10 copies of its DNA.

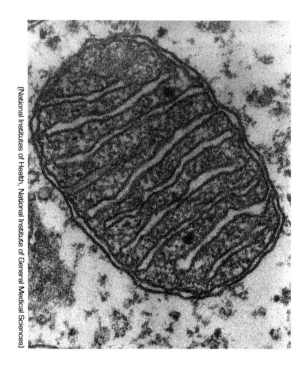

[National Institutes of Health, National Institute of General Medical Sciences]

A single mitochondrion. A human cell may have up to 100 mitochondria, depending on its energy needs.

Other Organelles

ATP (adenosine triphosphate) is another type of organelle. It stores the energy produced by mitochondria as chemical bonds. The cell uses the energy to produce proteins and nucleic acids or in order to move. Enzymes called ATPases release the energy from the ATP.

Ribosomes, particles that build proteins, are another type of organelle. Some ribosomes are attached to membranes called the *endoplasmic reticulum* and produce proteins to be secreted from the cell. Other ribosomes are free or unattached. They produce proteins that stay in the cell.

The *Golgi bodies* or *Golgi apparatus* are a series of cytoplasm membranes containing enzymes that tag or label outgoing proteins with "address labels" in the form of sugar molecules. These tags show the proteins' destinations.

Lysosomes are vacuoles (pockets) containing enzymes that break down large proteins that enter the cell.

The cells of a species or organ may have specialized organelles. For instance, plant cells that perform photosynthesis (make energy from sunlight) have special algaelike organelles called *plastids*.

Cell Membrane or Wall

The cytoplasm is surrounded by a three-layer cell wall (for plants) or membrane (other organisms). The inside layer, the cell cortex, is a structural material called actin that can form or dissolve polymers (long molecules), allowing the cell to change shape, move, and let molecules move between cells in a tissue.

The middle layer is a plasma membrane made of fats (lipids). It contains enzymes called ion channels that let chemicals in and out of the cell. The outer layer, the extracellular matrix, is a gluey substance made of sugars and proteins. It lets cells stick to each other.

Receptors

On the outer surface of the cell membrane are receptors—proteins that bind to specific molecules (attract and hold them), sometimes passing substances into the cell. Receptors are embedded in the cell membrane, with one end sticking into the cytoplasm and the other extending above the outside of the membrane.

Cell Cycle

The life of a cell—its "birth," growth, reproduction, and death—is called the *cell cycle.* It is composed of several phases.

G_1 is a period of growth preparation for DNA duplication. The actual duplicating of the cell's genetic material (DNA), called *synthesis*, is the S phase. G_2 is another period of growth and preparation for cell division. The division of the cell into two completely separate cells, called *mitosis*, is known as the M phase. The cycle also includes a quiescent (quiet or resting) phase, called G_0.

If the cell is a reproductive cell—an egg or sperm—the cycle is modified to allow for fertilization and the incorporation of both egg and sperm DNA in the new cell. Cell division in unfertilized reproductive cells—gametes—is called *meiosis.*

The phases are marked in two ways: time and a series of chemical signals. The markers start each phase, make sure it is being carried out correctly, and end it, so that the cell can begin the next phase.

In a many-celled organism, such as a human, events elsewhere in the organism determine whether and when the cell begins moving through the cycle phases. Once it begins, the cell controls its own activity.

The cell cycle also controls *cell differentiation.* This process turns a generalized cell, called a *stem cell,* into a specific one. For example, as an embryo develops, some cells become brain cells, some liver cells, and

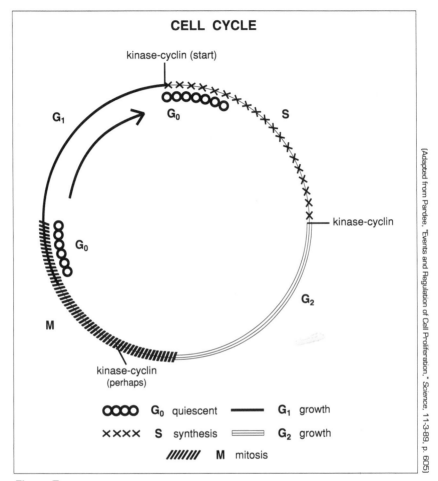

[Adapted from Pardee, "Events and Regulation of Cell Proliferation," *Science,* 11-3-89, p. 605]

Figure 7

so on. Differentiation also takes place in a mature person. For instance, some stem cells in the the bone marrow can become red blood cells.

Cancer is an abnormal form of cell division and differentiation.

How the Cell Cycle Operates

There used to be two cell-cycle theories, called "domino" and "clock." The "domino" theory said that each event in the cell cycle was triggered by the event that occurred before it. In turn, it set off the next event, like a series of falling dominoes. The "clock" theory said that each event occurred at a preset time in the cycle.

Scientists now know that the cell cycle progresses through a combination of domino and clock triggers. Cell-cycle events appear to take place within a certain time frame. But a chain reaction also occurs, and events are interdependent.

The force that drives the cell cycle is a protein partnership between two kinds of chemicals called *kinases* and *cyclins*.

The entire cell cycle is controlled by a set of genes called cell-division genes, or cdc genes. Each cdc gene instructs the cell to produce a kinase needed to operate the cycle.

Scientists are still discovering the exact process, but it appears that the kinase-cyclin partnership operates at several points in the cell cycle:

- during G_1 called start, when the cell may or may not proceed to the S phase;
- at the end of the S phase, when the cell may or may not begin mitosis or meiosis;
- possibly during the M phase, when the chromosomes prepare to divide.

The kinase-cyclin partnership is like a person who directs a movie and also stars in it. The partnership performs some operations itself and also controls the activity of proteins that perform other operations.

Other genes are active at cell-cycle decision points, either letting the cycle go on or, if there are signs of a problem, stopping it in its tracks.

Kinases

Cell-cycle kinases are proteins (enzymes) formed by a gene named cdc2. They take phosphate groups from ATP (the cell's energy storehouse) and add them to proteins, activating the proteins for cell-cycle work, such as copying DNA for cell reproduction. The main methods of controlling cell-cycle events are the addition of phosphates (called phosphorylation) and their removal with other enzymes called phosphatases.

Research has shown that the proteins produced by the cdc2 gene are virtually identical in yeast and in human cells. A scientist can splice human DNA into a yeast cell with an inactive cdc2 gene, and the gene will become active. A million years of evolution have left the gene practically unchanged.

Cyclins

The cell manufactures cyclins and stockpiles a certain amount. At this point the cyclins combine forces with a cdc kinase and the partnership goes to work. Different cyclins are formed for different parts of the cell cycle.

As the partnership works, the cyclin is gradually used up. When only a small amount is left, the phosphatase enzymes remove the phosphates that the kinases had added, and the partnership stops working. It goes back to work only when the amount of cyclin has been built up again.

In some species, simply putting kinase and cyclin together is enough to begin cell-cycle activity. Other species require a specific level of another protein, called cdc25.

Initial Growth and Preparation Phase (G₁)

G_1 is the phase of the cell cycle in which cells grow and also make RNA that will let them duplicate their DNA and divide.

Scientists used to think that the G_1 phase was just a period between the last cell division and the next DNA duplication. They now know that it is a series of about 16 overlapping events or steps that take place almost entirely in the cytoplasm. It may begin at the end of a previous cell cycle. Or it can come after a quiescent (quiet) state. In most cells G_1 takes about 12 hours to complete. But the phase takes a much shorter time in fertilized cells (early embryos).

Nutrients and chemicals that stimulate the cell to grow start and end each G_1 event. Some G_1 events can begin during other phases of the cell cycle. They can even start while other major processes, such as DNA duplication, are going on. The following description is based on one developed by Arthur Pardee of Harvard University:

Step 1 and Step 2 Small proteins called *growth factors* approach the cell and bind with growth-factor receptors on the cell membrane. These molecules group together within the cytoplasm.

Step 3 In the cytoplasm, signal-carrying chemicals prepare the cell to produce more cell proteins, which will be required when the cell copies itself.

Step 4 In the nucleus, proteins that regulate gene expression bind to DNA in the nucleus. They turn some genes on and others off.

Step 5 Molecules of an early form of RNA appear, showing that genes have been turned on.

Step 6 The early RNA is changed into the final form of RNA. Like a messenger, the RNA is sent into the cytoplasm where it makes proteins needed for cell division (*Step 7*), though scientists don't yet understand what they do.

Step 8 Special amino acids are brought into the cell to be built into protein later on.

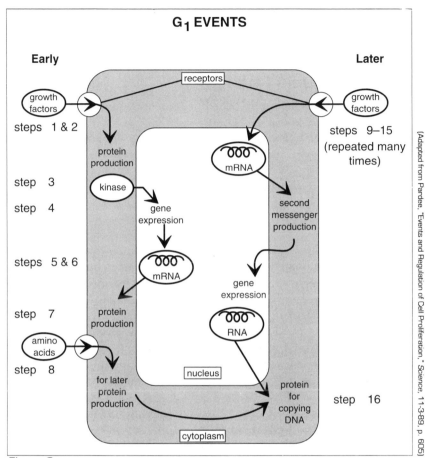

Figure 8

[Adapted from Pardee, "Events and Regulation of Cell Proliferation," *Science*, 11-3-89, p. 605]

Steps 9–15 Growth factors are brought into the cell to the nucleus, where more RNA is created and sent into the cytoplasm. This process stimulates other chemical messengers, called *second messengers*, which lead to more genes being turned on. This process is repeated several times.

Step 16 In this final step, the RNA sent into the cytoplasm uses the special amino acids (Step 8) to build enzymes on the ribosomes. These enzymes, in turn, move into the nucleus where they merge into the protein that will actually make the DNA copy. At the same time, the cell also produces enzymes that will uncoil the DNA at the point where replication will begin.

These events provide the organization and materials to begin the next phase of the cell cycle, the copying of nuclear DNA so that the cell can divide.

DNA Synthesis Phase (S)

In this phase of the cell cycle, which lasts a few hours, the cell that has completed the G_1 phase makes an exact copy of its DNA—a process called *replication*. This process involves copying four components:

- the DNA itself
- the nucleosomes—chromatin consisting of DNA and another chemical called histone
- the scaffolding that supports the DNA
- in many species, copying whether the gene is on (active) or off (inactive)

Human DNA consists of approximately 3 billion base pairs in 23 pairs of chromosomes. Scientists have watched the copying process and found that it works at a rate of 3,000 bases (3 kb) per minute. If just one replication cycle were carried out for the entire human DNA, it would take a little less than two years!

In reality, for most species replication starts at many DNA sites at the same time. All replications do not start or finish at the same time. For example, active genes are usually copied early in S phase.

The entire process takes less than a day. In a normal cell, it must be done very accurately if the next cell generation is to be normal too. If replication of a human chromosome is not complete, when the cell splits, the chromosome will break, causing a genetic defect. Substitution of nucleotides is another type of mistake that can occur, also causing a genetic defect.

During any eukaryotic cell cycle, replication occurs just once. (This is not the case in prokaryotes.) Scientists have found that cytoplasm from cells of one species that have completed G_1 can cause replication in cells of another species. But if the cells have completed the S phase, the replication in the new species won't take place.

Copying the DNA

The replication process involves a *replication fork*, a complex protein that untwists the DNA helix and separates the two strands. Each strand is copied so that the new strand is its complement, or mirror image. In other words, the copying molecule reads each A,

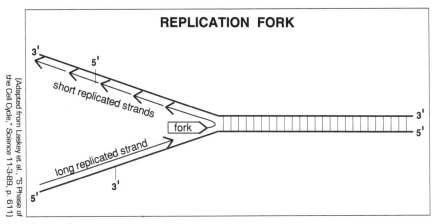

[Adapted from Laskey et al. "S Phase of the Cell Cycle." *Science* 11-3-89, p. 611]

Figure 9

C, G, or T, and manufactures a copy of its mirror image—the base on the other side of the rung. For example, if the copier reads a C, it makes G. If it reads T, it makes A. If the original strand has a section that reads ACATG, the new section will read TGTAC.

Within a chromosome, replication follows the fork on one strand, producing a long section of new bases. On the other strand, the replication moves in the opposite direction and produces a series of short sections. Replication always begins at a 5' location and ends at a 3'(so called because of its attachment position on the backbone sugar molecule). Replication ends when a special enzyme copies the *telomere*, which is the end structure of a chromosome.

Copying the DNA–Related Structures
Following right behind the replication fork is the enzyme that assembles the new DNA into nucleosomes.

While the scaffolding is made of proteins, scientists haven't yet found out how it is replicated. Scientists also don't know whether the nuclear skeleton freezes the DNA in place or whether it is somehow attached to the chromosome scaffolding. But some kind of skeletal structure seems to be part of the process.

Second Growth and Preparation Phase (G2)
After the cell has copied the members of its community, it goes through another period of growth and preparation for the cell splitting.

Mitosis or Meiosis Phase (M)

Now that all the parts of the cell have duplicated themselves, if the cell commits itself to splitting into two cells, the process begins. This process can take one of two forms. Mitosis is the splitting process for all cells except those used in sexual reproduction—sperm and egg. The counterpart for reproductive cells is meiosis.

Mitosis

Mitosis comes from the Greek word meaning thread. The phases of mitosis are:

- *Prophase:* The duplicate sets of chromosomes become shorter and thicker and begin to move toward the nuclear membrane. A structure called a *spindle* forms. The nuclear membrane breaks down.
- *Metaphase:* The chromosomes—the original ones and the ones replicated during S phase—cluster at midspindle.
- *Anaphase:* The two sets of chromosomes separate. The cell becomes elongated with a bulge at each end, looking very much like a peanut in the shell.
- *Telophase:* The chromosomes begin to lengthen. New nuclear membranes form around each set of chromosomes.
- *Cytokinesis:* Half of the cytoplasm and organelles form around each new nucleus. The mitochondria are distributed randomly between the two.
- Finally, a cellular membrane forms around each new cell, completing the process of mitosis. Now there are two daughter cells, each the same size as the original cell at the beginning of the cycle.

Meiosis

Meiosis is the process of cell division for those cells that will become eggs and sperm. A variation of mitosis, meiosis goes through the prophase, metaphase, anaphase, and telophase. Meiosis must produce cells with half the ordinary number of chromosomes. When the sperm and egg unite in fertilization, the cells of the resulting embryo will have the normal number of chromosomes—half from each parent.

The male reproductive cell begins as a spermatocyte. It undergoes meiosis only after the male is sexually mature. The cell contains the full number of non-sex chromosomes, called autosomes. It also has an X chromosome and a Y chromosome. In

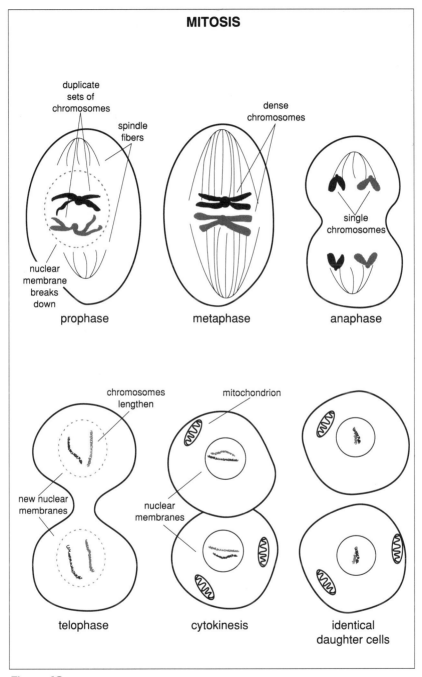

MITOSIS

duplicate sets of chromosomes

spindle fibers

dense chromosomes

nuclear membrane breaks down

single chromosomes

prophase

metaphase

anaphase

chromosomes lengthen

mitochondrion

new nuclear membranes

nuclear membranes

telophase

cytokinesis

identical daughter cells

Figure 10

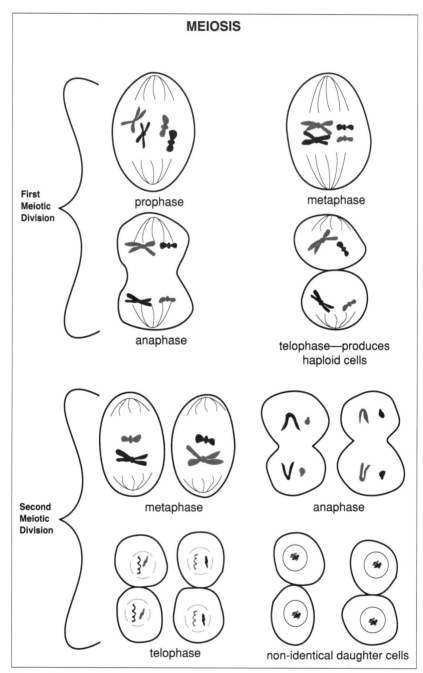

Figure 11

humans, the total number of chromosomes is 46. The cell splits twice in the process of meiosis.

In the male cell's first meiotic division, it splits without having duplicated its DNA. This produces two haploid cells—cells with half the usual number of chromosomes. One haploid cell has the X chromosome and the other one has the Y chromosome. Each of these cells doubles itself in an S phase and then, in the second meiotic division, splits. The result is four sperm, two carrying an X chromosome and two with a Y chromosome. Each also has 22 autosomes.

The female cell begins meiosis before the female carrying it is even born. The cell begins as an oocyte (egg cell) in the ovary. The human oocyte has 23 pairs of chromosomes, including two X chromosomes. In the first meiotic division, the oocyte forms a small bulge called a polar body. One of each pair of chromosomes remains in the main cell. The rest of the chromosomes cluster in the polar body, which separates and is discarded. In mammals, this occurs shortly before birth.

The rest of meiosis takes place when the female becomes sexually mature. As the egg is readied to leave the ovary (ovulation), it goes through the S phase. Each chromosome makes a copy of itself. The egg cell begins to form a second polar body. In the second meiotic division, one of each chromosome pair collects in each part of the cell. The large cell is the egg ready to receive a sperm.

If the sperm and egg unite, the second polar body is discarded. When the sperm nucleus and the egg nucleus merge, the new embryo has a set of chromosome pairs, half from the sperm and half from the egg.

The new embryo goes through chromosome replication and mitosis without growth phases, a process known as cleavage. Then it begins a regular cell cycle.

Quiescent Phase (G_0)

The quiescent phase is the phase in which cells no longer divide, or take a break before resuming the cycle. Cells get smaller because they use up their protein and RNA and rebuild them at only about one-third as fast as in other phases. Scientists say that the growth of a population of cells depends on the number of cells in phase G_0 in relation to the number of cells in G_1.

The Cell at Work

In the S phase of the cell cycle, DNA's helix shape is temporarily straightened out while the bases are copied. The helix shape is also straightened out when a gene is copied into RNA, so that the RNA can make a protein. The copying process is called *transcription.* A gene can be copied once or many times, depending on how much protein the cell must make.

Transcription

In transcription, an enzyme called an *RNA polymerase* temporarily straightens out the needed segment of nuclear DNA. It reads each A, C, G, or T and makes a copy of its mirror image, substituting U for T. This means that the DNA base series ATCGAA will be copied as RNA UAGCUU. When the new strand of RNA is complete, the DNA twists back into a helix once again.

If the DNA molecule contained only instructions, the copying process would be done and the RNA could move to a ribosome (protein-manufacturing area) in the cytoplasm and start making proteins. But DNA is more complicated. Some nucleotides don't carry instructions. These nucleotides may be meaningless—what scientists sometimes call junk—or they may have as-yet unknown purposes. So the RNA goes through two steps called *maturation* and *translation.*

The RNA produced by transcription—the first step—is called pre-messenger RNA (pre-mRNA). It has two classes of nucleotides:

- *exons*—the instructions
- *introns*—the noninstructional nucleotides

Maturation

During the next step, *maturation*, the introns are deleted, or removed, with enzymes, the exons are pasted together, and three things are added:

- A nucleotide sequence at the beginning of the RNA molecule called a *cap.* The beginning is usually referred to as 5'.
- A series of nucleotides containing many adenines (As), known as a *poly A sequence*, at the end of the molecule (its 3' location).
- An *AUG* codon, a password to the ribosome. It insures that the first amino acid built at the ribosome is methionine.

When maturation is complete, the molecule has become *messenger RNA* (*mRNA*) and moves from the nucleus to a ribosome in the cytoplasm.

Translation

In the process called *translation*, the ribosome reads and follows the RNA's instructions for protein production. A ribosome itself is made of RNA and protein. The cytoplasm also contains transfer RNA (tRNA) codons, each with its amino acid attached.

A ribosome reads the first mRNA codon, AUG, and joins it with the tRNA that has the amino acid methionine attached. Methionine acts as a starting location for the rest of the amino acids specified in the mRNA. The ribosome moves along the mRNA, joining each codon to the appropriate tRNA. When the ribosome has read all the mRNA codons and joined them to tRNAs, the protein is complete.

If many copies of the DNA have been transcribed into RNA, ribosomes can read them all at the same time. Also, the protein production process may be more like an assembly line. It is possible that a series of ribosomes moves along the same RNA sequence, one after another, reading its instructions and making the protein.

Another time when the DNA helix is read and copied is when the cell has been damaged and needs fixing.

Cell Maintenance and Repair

Damage to a cell's DNA can come from a variety of sources outside of the cell or the organism, or from within it. Examples include toxic substances and ultraviolet radiation from the sun. If the damage is not too great, the cell can repair the DNA, using some of the same enzymes that duplicate the DNA before the cell divides into two.

Enzymes that routinely take part in DNA replication also find and, if possible, correct damaged nucleotides. The same enzymes also find and correct errors made during the duplication of the DNA before dividing.

Such enzymes routinely patrol the chromosomes, looking for problem sites. When a damaged or incorrect sequence is found, the enzyme attaches to the site and signals for additional enzymes to come and help with the repair. The reinforced enzyme snips out the damaged sequence and discards it.

Still other enzymes assemble a copy of the original sequence, filling in the gap by reading the undamaged nucleotides on the other strand, then making their complements (mirror images), such as reading G and making C.

Repairs are performed mostly on chromosome areas containing large numbers of active genes or on those that are switched on and off frequently—those on the outside of the twisted DNA molecule.

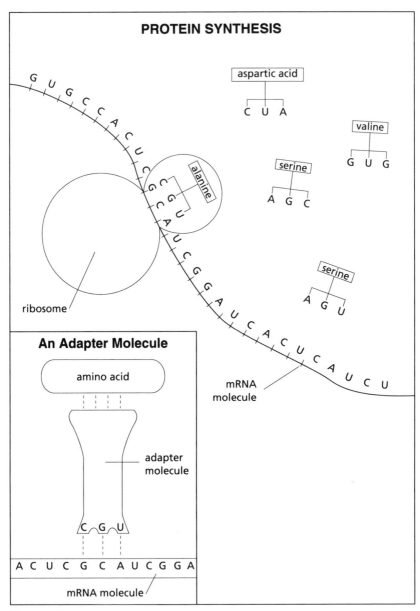

Figure 12

If the damage is too great, or if the damage is in areas with few genes or inactive ones, the DNA may produce incorrect signals or chemicals, causing illness to the organism or a mutation in the next generation of cells. Or the cell may divide abnormally, starting the process of changing into a cancer cell.

Scientists are still learning things about the way cells and their DNA work. Even so, there is enough information for genetic engineers to take these basic natural processes and adapt them for human control and use.

Fruits and vegetables, cattle and other animals, criminal investigation, and medical treatments have all been changed through genetic engineering. The next chapters will describe developments in all these fields.

3 GENETIC ENGINEERING IN AGRICULTURE

In the 17th century it was the black tulip. In the 1860s it was the garden pea. In the 1980s it was the super petunia. Agriculture and genetics have been partners throughout scientific history to control plants' reproduction and create new products. Today genetic engineering of plants and animals has allowed changes that are meant to bring people better and more healthful food, a safer and more pleasant environment, and improvements in health.

All these changes are based on a series of techniques developed from the processes of natural cells and their DNA. These techniques, which will be discussed in the following chapters, include recombinant DNA, polymerase chain reaction (PCR), cell cultures, monoclonal antibodies, and nucleic acid hybridization.

Every new technology brings risks and frightens some people, whether it's new energy sources, new machinery, or new ways of farming. Genetic engineering brings risks as well as benefits. Because the field is so new, some people think the techniques need to be used even more carefully. Others want genetic engineering to be applied, widely, like any other new tool. This chapter discusses the controversies along with the techniques.

Genetic Engineering in Animals

Cattle have been domesticated since the dawn of history for meat, milk, or both. They were among species to be brought in from the wild. Pastoralism, in which whole societies are built around the herding, moving, and grazing of cattle or other animals, was one of the major transitions from hunting and gathering to permanent settlements. Some traditional cultures still practice pastoralism.

The many breeds of cattle existing today can be traced to intentional or selective breeding begun hundreds of years ago. Cattle breeders have made use of the principles of genetics as they have been uncovered. The pedigrees and breeding of today's dairy cattle are as carefully chosen and recorded as those of racehorses and royalty.

Cattle breeders were among the first to use sperm banks and artificial insemination. Cattle feed is also scientifically formulated, and cattle routinely get nutritional supplements and antibiotics to reduce the chance of illness and premature death.

Today the dairy industry is one of the leaders in biotechnology, including genetic engineering. One technique involves genetically engineered cattle genes.

Transgenic Animals

Transgenic is one of those words that used to show up in science fiction but is now part of everyday life. The term means **trans**planted **gen**es from one organism to another—what are called foreign genes. Sometimes the gene comes from another plant or animal of the same species. But genes also have been moved between animal species, between plant species, and even from animal to plant. Later generations of the organism then inherit the new gene.

All sorts of genes can be transplanted. One example is a set of genes that does a better job of controlling the immune system's defense against bacteria and viruses. Another is genes that make an animal or plant grow larger or faster, or both. Canadian scientists have found that flounder, a fish that lives in the very cold waters of the Atlantic Ocean, produce an antifreeze. The scientists have transplanted the antifreeze gene into salmon, to allow salmon to be farmed in colder climates.

In cattle, genes could be inserted to reduce the amount of fat in meat. According to the U.S. Department of Agriculture, genes that protect cattle or other meat animals against disease could reduce the amount of antibiotics they are fed. This would make the meat more healthful for people to eat.

Disease prevention is important too. Mastitis is a common, costly, and painful inflammation of a cow's udder. One company has designed a protein produced by bacteria that can be sprayed on the cow's teats to prevent the disease.

Genetic techniques are already being used to breed cattle whose milk contains superior cheese-making proteins. The same techniques

Scientists are developing chickens that mature faster and produce more meat. They are also working to enhance disease-resistance. Here, animal geneticist Lyman Crittenden and technician Leonard Provencher check chickens maintained in plastic canopy isolators to test for viruses. In the future, scientists may be able to manipulate the germs that threaten chickens as well as the birds themselves.

are used to identify human genetic diseases, such as sickle-cell anemia and some types of cancer.

Making Animals Transgenic

Scientists transplant the foreign gene into animals by inserting it into a fertilized egg, as discussed below. Depending on the species, the egg matures and hatches, or it is inserted into a surrogate mother, matures and is born. In plants, scientists introduce the gene into a cell that is then grown into a whole plant in a method called *cloning*.

Transgenic methods of breeding cattle and other animals are beginning to replace traditional methods. These methods are also used in medical research. Laboratory animals become living disease models when the gene responsible for a disease is inserted into them and inherited by the next generation. The gene then causes the disease in the animals as it would in a human, allowing scientists to experiment with methods of treatment and prevention.

The basic method of transplanting a gene is adapted from what DNA and RNA are doing naturally all the time. There are four steps to the process.

Gene Preparation

As discussed earlier, in the process of preparing RNA in the nucleus, the first step is copying the DNA, including noncoding sequences (introns). These introns are then cut out and the information sequences are pasted together. In genetic engineering, this cut-and-paste method is called *gene splicing*.

First scientists identify the wanted gene; one way of doing this is by using a linkage map. They then cut out the section of DNA that contains the gene, using *restriction enzymes* (or *restriction endonucleases*). These are the same kind of enzymes used to remove introns from RNA, and they have the ability to identify specific sequences and make cuts as necessary.

Once the gene is cut out, it needs to be sent into the target or host cell. Again, nature provides the carrier (also called a *vector*)—a bacteria. Bacteria are single-celled organisms that can move into a cell. In nature, bacteria move into cells to find a home and food. For genetic engineering, the bacteria's harmful abilities are removed or turned off.

Many bacteria species contain circular DNA molecules called *plasmids*. A plasmid is cut with the same enzymes used to remove the desired gene. This means the plasmid is cut at comparable locations. The desired gene sequence is then pasted into place with another enzyme, called *DNA ligase*.

Now the *recombinant plasmid*, the plasmid in which the DNA has been recombined, is inserted into a bacterium. The process is repeated many times. Then the altered bacteria are grown into a large colony. Because the recombination process doesn't always succeed, not all the members of the colony actually carry the recombinant DNA plasmid. To separate the carriers, a *probe* is used. This probe is a DNA sequence that homes in on a specific location, such as the desired gene. Scientists tag the probe with a radioactive element or by some other method, so that it can be identified.

Variations of this method include making exact copies of the DNA (clones) or using a virus instead of a bacteria as the carrier.

Now that the foreign gene is ready, the host cell—an embryo—must be prepared.

Preparing the Host Cell

The gene transfer method isn't very efficient, meaning that many cells must be used to assure a successful transfer. The ovaries of mammals contain tens of thousands of eggs, many more than would ever be used in nature. This fact allows use of a process called *superovulation*.

For example, to make a transgenic cow, one cow is given hormones to make her shed 10 eggs instead of the usual one. These eggs are fertilized in the laboratory, but many embryos die at an early stage.

Research into improving control of the reproductive cycle of the cows providing the host cells is also valuable in timing the reproductive cycle of the surrogate mother cow, a second cow in whose womb the embryo will be implanted.

A different technique under development uses stem cells from the embryo as the vectors, or carriers. These undifferentiated cells can be stimulated to differentiate. This technique is a step forward because stem cells home in on specific locations—for instance, a cell that is "told" to be a muscle cell goes to the muscle. This process lets the new genes replace the existing ones in the host cell.

The method involves removing cells from an early embryo and growing them in the laboratory, refining the process until only stem cells are being grown. The desired DNA is then spliced in, and then the cells are injected into the embryo to be transplanted. The technique has been successful so far in mice, hamsters, rabbits, and swine.

Transferring the Gene

The first transgenic animals were mice. They were engineered by using an egg that was fertilized so recently that the sperm nucleus and the egg nucleus hadn't yet merged. This embryo was removed from the mouse. Cloned DNA was injected into the sperm nucleus. Then the embryo was inserted into a surrogate mother.

Transfer can also be done using viruses as the vectors of the cloned DNA. Both techniques have been used to produce transgenic cattle, pigs, sheep, and chickens.

Duplicating and Transferring the Embryo

The final step before implantation in the surrogate is to duplicate the embryo. In the original method—now widely used in the transplanting of natural cattle embryos—the embryo was split in half, turning it into identical twins. Each half can also be split, producing four embryos for every successful engineering. If the embryo is divided more than twice, however, too many embryos die.

Another duplication method is *nuclear transplantation*. In this process an embryo cell's nucleus is transplanted into an egg whose own nucleus has been removed. An electrical pulse fuses the embryo nucleus into its new cell. The engineered embryo can then

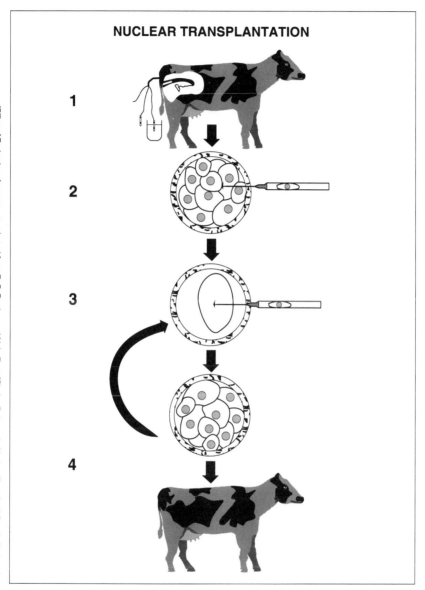

(Office of Technology Assessment, adapted from R. S. Prather and N. L. First, "Cloning Embryos by Nuclear Transfer," *Genetic Engineering in Animals*, W. Hansell and B. J. Weir (eds.), *Journal of Reproduction and Fertility Ltd.*, Cambridge, U.K., 1990, pp. 125–134.)

Figure 13: (1) An embryo is nonsurgically removed from a donor cow or is produced by in vitro fertilization. (2) Individual embryo cells are removed. (3) Each embryo cell is injected into a specially prepared egg cell that has had its nucleus removed. An electric pulse is administered to cause fusion. (4) Each cell is grown to a multicell embryo, at which point the cloning procedure can be repeated or the embryo can be transplanted to a cow that eventually gives birth.

be grown and the process repeated, or it can be implanted into a surrogate.

Problems with the Technique

As with any new technology, problems can develop. It is hard to pinpoint the engineered gene's target location accurately. Also, it's not yet possible to control whether a gene is turned on or off. If a gene is inserted in the "on" position, it may function all the time, instead of just at specific times.

Another problem is questions about safety—of humans as well as animals. The following example shows one kind of potential danger.

Bovine Growth Hormone and Milk Production

Dairy researchers want to add another way to today's breeding techniques to make dairy cows more productive and more economical. The family dairy farm exists, but most milk production is performed on a large scale. Dairying is an industry—and big business. In 1989, for instance, American dairy products earned $19.3 billion.

Every aspect of milk production, from conception of calves to the sale of the milk, is highly controlled by economics and governmental regulation. The cattle themselves are commodities, or perhaps factory machinery. When their useful milk-producing life is past, they are sold, often for fast-food hamburgers.

For many years, dairy farmers have produced more milk and milk products than the market can absorb. The U.S. government buys this surplus and uses it to supply school lunch and welfare programs.

The profit margin on milk is very slim. If dairy farmers want to make money, they must produce as much milk as possible but with as few cows as possible. And each cow should begin producing milk as soon as possible.

One way to make a cow give more milk is to increase the amount of a growth hormone that will make each cow produce as much as 12 percent more milk. The hormone is called bovine somatotropin (bST)—the word means tissue growth. It is sometimes called bovine growth hormone (bGH). Unlike breeding improvements, which could take 10 to 20 years, bST's effect is immediate.

Essentially, a more productive animal is one that makes more efficient use of the food it eats. Somatotropin is a natural protein

Animal physiologist Dr. Vernon Pursel of the Agricultural Research Service-USDA examines a pig born with a bovine growth hormone gene inserted in the embryo through genetic engineering. Through research on gene insertions, scientists hope to produce leaner and faster-growing pigs using less feed.

produced by the pituitary gland, and it is a key regulator of growth. It also increases the amount of milk produced by a lactating female, the ability that made bST attractive to dairy researchers. The hormone works whether it is produced by the animal's own pituitary gland or is injected into the animal.

The idea of giving cows additional bST has been around for decades. Research began in the late 1930s. Until the early 1980s, bST could be made only from the pituitary glands of slaughtered animals. But now, recombinant bST (rbST, also called recombinant bovine growth factor, rbGH) is available.

Recombinant bST

In nature, a gene directs bST production. To make recombinant bST, the gene is cloned in the laboratory, then inserted into bacteria. Large colonies of the bacteria produce the hormone. The recombinant production method has had two effects: It greatly reduced the price of bST, and it has made the hormone very controversial.

The low-cost production method means that bST could be made in large amounts and sold to a mass market. But genetic engineering is a new technology. New technologies always require a lot of research time and money before they can begin to produce savings for buyers and profits for the manufacturers.

rbST is the first agricultural biotechnology substance with wide economic importance. Its success will pave the way for many more recombinant products to follow. Four major chemical companies—Monsanto Chemical Company, Eli Lilly and Company, Upjohn Corporation, and American Cyanamid Corporation—have been developing rbST since the late 1970s and have spent $500 million on it. But estimates for worldwide sales range from $100 million to $1 billion a year.

rbST needs just one thing before it can be put on the market—approval from the governments of the countries where it will be used. In the United States, the Food and Drug Administration (FDA) will decide whether rbST is safe. This is where the controversy comes.

The Controversy

There are four variants of the natural bST molecule, each composed of either 190 or 191 amino acids. Like all somatotropins, bST must bind to specific receptors in the body in order to work. Recombinant bST may be like one of the four variants. Or it may differ from all of them. In the manufacturing process, the bacterial ribosomes may add one to eight extra amino acids at the end of the molecule. Still, the amino acid sequence and the folding of the molecule are the same as in a natural bST. The safety of each recombinant variation is being studied. Supporters, including the four chemical companies plus some large dairy cooperatives, believe rbST will make dairying more efficient and provide consumers with lower-price milk.

Approval Process

The chemical companies have applied to the FDA for approval to sell rbST. In 1985 the FDA said rbST was safe and allowed its use in experiments with dairy herds around the country. Milk from these herds is mixed with other milk and sold in the commercial milk market. Now the FDA must decide whether it can be used and sold generally.

Opposition

Opponents have several objections to rbST. They think that it will:

- increase milk supplies and drive milk prices lower,
- change the image of milk as a wholesome natural product, and
- drive many dairy farmers out of business.

The earliest opponent of rbST was Jeremy Rifkin, who started the Foundation on Economic Trends to oppose many applications of biotechnology on safety grounds. He began opposing the approval and use of rbST in 1986.

Despite the commercialization of dairy farming, many family dairy farmers still exist. Like the large dairy farmers, the farm families make only a small profit. But dairying is their way of life. Many of them oppose the introduction of rbST, because they fear the new technology will be too costly for them, so they won't be able to compete in the marketplace.

The small farmers are supported by some small dairy cooperatives, which market milk, and by the 300,000 member National Farmers Union. According to various surveys, up to 80 percent of dairy farmers oppose the use of rbST.

Several state legislatures oppose the use of rbST, as do some foreign countries. The Netherlands has banned research. And the European Parliament has recommended strict limits on its use.

In 1991 Consumers Union, which publishes *Consumer Reports*, questioned the safety of rbST. Various dairies have decided not to use milk that comes from rbST-treated cows. But it is still unclear who is right and whether rbST is safe or unsafe.

Safety

Everyone agrees that a growth hormone must be used carefully. For instance, in any species a deficiency in growth hormone can cause dwarfism. Too much can cause arthritis and other bone problems. In normal animals, including people, growth hormone is produced only when required to start or maintain growth.

And rbST does have a built-in safety factor for humans. Because of the shape of the somatotropin molecule and the way it must link up with receptors in the body, the somatotropin made by each species is specific to that species or, at most, to closely- related species. For example, the cattle version of somatotropin is also active in sheep, a closely related species. But it doesn't work in humans.

The controversy centers on another hormone, whose level rises with the amount of rbST in the blood. This hormone, called insulinlike growth factor-1 (IGF-1), is found in the milk. People's blood normally has 200 µg/liter of insulinlike growth factor. The milk of cows treated with rbST has about 20 µg/liter.

Some opponents say this makes bST a health and safety issue, because people who drink the milk will take in additional IGF-1.

Supporters say that the digestive process breaks down the IGF-1 in milk after it is consumed, so that little of it gets into the blood. They also say that the increased amount is too small to worry about, compared with the amount occurring naturally in human blood.

Consumers Union wants the FDA to reexamine its 1985 approval of the safety of rbST, on the basis of the higher-than-normal levels of the IGF-1 that are found in milk from cows treated with rbST. Consumers Union also wants the FDA to examine the possibility that cows given rbST might need higher levels of antibiotics, which could also get into the milk.

Some leading scientists say rbST is safe, mainly because it is not active in humans. In 1990 Congress asked the National Institutes of Health (NIH) to look into the safety of rbST.

The NIH convened a panel of experts called a consensus conference—a highly unusual thing to do. The NIH often convenes such groups *after* the FDA approves a drug's use, to recommend how new drugs should be used. The rbST conference was different, since it was convened *before* approval.

The NIH experts concluded that milk and meat from cattle treated with rbST are as safe as those from untreated cattle. Although the amount of IGF-1 in cows treated with rbST is double that in untreated cows, the increase in humans who consume beef and dairy products is too minute to have an effect. Human saliva contains a much larger amount of IGF-1 than that found in milk from rbST-treated cows. The experts played down future problems, but they called for more studies of the human health effects.

Another possible problem is harm to the gastrointestinal tract, including the esophagus, of newborn babies. But newborns are rarely fed whole cow's milk. And in any case, the level of IGF-1 in milk from rbST-treated cows is only slightly higher than that in human breast milk.

But the NIH scientists said more research is needed on the possible relationship between rbST and increased risk of mastitis in dairy cows. Another possible problem is increased infertility. To treat these problems, the cattle will be receiving antibiotics and fertility drugs that they otherwise wouldn't. If these drugs stay in the cows' bodies, they could mean an additional risk to human health.

Other safety questions:

- Can rbST cause allergic reactions in people? The FDA says the risk is extremely small and that people are exposed to many common foods that cause allergies, including milk.
- rbST builds muscle. Could athletes misuse the drug? The FDA says because rbST is inactive in humans, misuse is unlikely.

- Does the possible increase in antibiotics in cows' milk pose any risk to humans? According to the FDA, existing regulations will prevent any possible overexposure to antibiotics. Still, some critics say that the levels of antibiotics in cows' milk are already too high and should be more strictly regulated by the FDA.

Social and Economic Priorities
Critics are also asking:

- Why was rbST selected to be the first one to get the big commercial push in agriculture, when milk is in such oversupply already?
- Will its use simply result in production of more milk that the government will have to purchase as a surplus?
- Finally, why didn't the agriculture industry decide to support a genetically engineered remedy for a more realistic public need, such as controlling cattle growth to produce leaner meat?

Vaccines and Diagnostics

Vaccines are substances that act like a disease by triggering an immune response against it. But they don't cause the illness. Later, if vaccinated people or animals come into contact with that disease, their body can fight it off. Scientists have developed recombinant vaccines for both bacterial and viral infections of farm animals. A natural mutant of the common intestinal bacteria *E. coli* has been found to prevent certain bacterial infections in cattle and pigs. Salmonella—which in its natural state can cause food poisoning—has also been modified for use.

The first recombinant vaccine against a viral infection was designed to protect against vesicular stomatitis, a disease of cattle, horses, and pigs. It causes fever and growths in the mouth and on the tongue. The vaccine consists of a protective gene and the virus vaccinia, which carries the protective gene into the animal's cells.

Vaccinia is the same virus that was the basis for the vaccine against the human disease smallpox. In fact, the word *vaccine* means "from cows." It was coined in the late 18th century to describe the original smallpox vaccine, which was made from the related and mild cattle disease called cowpox.

Before it is used as a carrier, vaccinia is inactivated by removing its own disease-causing genes. The protective gene is then inserted into it. After injection into the animal, the altered gene stimulates the immune response.

Similar genetic engineering methods have been used to create vaccines against rabies and rinderpest (a cattle disease with symptoms like stomach flu).

Scientists turn a disease organism into a vaccine by removing some genetic material (a process called *deletion*), making it weaker. The first commercial vaccine created by gene deletion was for a usually fatal disease of baby pigs called pseudorabies, which causes inflammation of the brain.

Vaccines against cattle diseases are also being developed by inserting genes that produce protective antigen into the same viruses that normally cause the diseases. Herpes and adenovirus are two examples.

Genetic Engineering in Plants

Plants are the subject of genetic engineering research for many of the same reasons animals are. In the early 1980s, a disease-fighting petunia

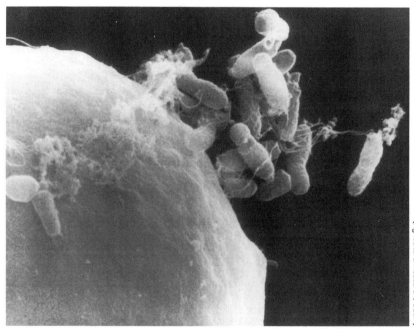

Scanning electron microscopy reveals several Agrobacterium tumefaciens *as they begin to infect a carrot cell. In the process, the bacteria's genetic material will enter the plant cell.* Agrobacterium *is often used to transfer a foreign gene into the plant being studied.*

(Agricultural Research, USDA)

became the first genetically engineered plant. Today food crops as well as decorative plants are being developed in genetic laboratories around the world. The technique is a lot like the one used in animals. The gene for a desirable trait is spliced into a bacterium, then introduced into a plant cell. The improved cell can then be grown into a new plant.

Agrobacterium tumefaciens is the bacteria species often used to transfer a foreign gene to a plant. To become the workhorse of plant genetic engineering, the bacteria also has been altered. In nature, it has a gene for crown gall, a disease that produces underground tumors in many species of plants. The strain of *Agrobacterium* used in the laboratory lacks that gene.

Genetic engineering can also be used to create hybrid plants, such as rice or tomatoes. Today, creating hybrids requires a lot of hand labor. Plants normally reproduce by pollinating nearby plants or by self-pollination. To make hybrids, workers must first remove the plants' pollen-producing organs by hand. Then the desired pollen can be introduced. A genetic technique has been studied to insert genes that prevent pollen development without harming the plant. This

[Agricultural Research, USDA]

Plant physiologist Freddi Hammerschlag examines a vial containing bacteria-resistant peach shoots grown from cells. Plants can be cloned from a single cell or bits of tissue. The cloning technique is essential in genetic engineering research because it can be used to multiply the number of altered cells quickly.

[Agricultural Research, USDA]

Surrounded by drought-dried cornstalks, drought-resistant lima beans prosper in a USDA test plot. If genetic engineers can isolate the genes that give the bean plants a high degree of drought tolerance, they could be transferred to other plants.

[Agricultural Research, USDA]

Natural pesticides at work—entomologist Hollis Flint compares an insect-ravaged cotton leaf from a control variety with one that has been genetically engineered with a protective gene from Bacillus thuringiensis.

would allow the plant to breed with other, better pollen, but without the manual pollen-removal step.

Soybeans are an important crop in the United States. Genetic techniques are being studied to improve their ability to use nitrogen, which will increase their production of several amino acids that are important in human nutrition. The hole in the earth's ozone layer admits increased amounts of ultraviolet radiation. Research has shown that this radiation can destroy a plant's protein. Some types of soybeans have a gene that protects against ultraviolet radiation, and scientists hope to use it to protect many types of crops.

Other uses of genetic engineering include making fruits and vegetables resistant to bruises during machine harvesting and improving the efficiency of a plant's photosynthesis—the process that uses sunlight to produce carbohydrates. The U.S. Department of Agriculture is studying an improved potato containing a chicken gene that fights bacteria and a moth bacteria that prevents bruises.

(Agricultural Research, USDA)

Plant geneticist Gene Galletta (left) and plant physiologist John Mass evaluate the yield and quality of the disease-resistant strawberry plants they are breeding. Galletta says, "If all pesticides were banned tomorrow, we'd lose only about 20 percent of the crop to pests and diseases we couldn't control. Many other crops could be completely wiped out."

Pesticides are also being engineered. One technique turns viruses into pesticides. This process is being used or planned for use against the tree pest gypsy moth and also against the pests that attack various vegetables. The advantage of these genetically engineered pesticides is that they affect only their specific target; they don't harm the environment.

Another type of pesticide is an anticaterpillar gene introduced into the cells of walnut trees from the natural pesticide *Bacillus thuringiensis*. The gene produces a protein that kills the early stage of moth pests. By using this pesticide, much smaller amounts of synthetic pesticides are expected to be needed when walnuts are stored.

Genetically Engineered Plants and the Natural Environment

In just a year or two, genetic engineering will bring to crops changes that used to take decades. Some ecologists suggest a cautious use of these techniques until their environmental consequences are known. One of these scientists is Norman Ellstrand, an ecological geneticist at the University of California, Riverside. He warns that what is good for crops could also turn out to be good for weeds, which would be bad for the environment.

Domestication of plants has always concentrated on dwarfing (making them smaller), making them productive without a dormant (inactive) period, and, for grains, retaining their seeds. But now, Ellstrand says, bioengineering is concentrating on the traits of resistance to herbicides, frost, and disease. These traits would benefit weeds as well as crop plants. Ellstrand's research has shown that pollen grains can travel for almost three-fourths of a mile. If engineered pollen blows far from the farm field, it could end up hybridizing weeds. Superweeds harmful to the environment and to the economy could develop.

Ellstrand recommends isolating fields with engineered crops, staggering the times when the new crops flower and put out pollen, and designing the crops so that the gene works in the farm field but is self-destructive if it escapes into the wild.

Genetic engineering is expected to become extremely important to farmers in the next few years. It has already become an important technique at the courthouse and the police station. The next chapter discusses the use of genetic techniques in identification and criminal investigation.

4 GENETIC FINGERPRINTING— DNA IN THE COURTROOM

For a century, just one part of the human body could identify an individual well enough to be used in a courtroom— the pattern of ridges on the fingerpads called fingerprints. Now another identifier has been accepted for legal use: DNA, a genetic fingerprint.

The method, more formally named *DNA typing*, is being called the most powerful tool yet developed for discovering genetic variation. It's based on the theory that each person has unique segments of DNA—they are different from anyone else's. The U.S. Department of Defense is now keeping DNA samples for every man and woman in military service. It's also used in everything from fossil identification to tracking zoo animal parentage.

But the biggest uses are in the courtroom—identifying the fathers of human babies and identifying criminals who commit violent crimes, such as murder and rape.

The heart of genetic fingerprinting is the ability to home in on segments of cell DNA that vary from individual to individual, snip them from the rest of the DNA, and make images of them that can be seen with the naked eye and compared. For instance, the DNA of a child and possible father may be compared, or DNA in a possible murderer's tissue sample found on a victim.

Preparing DNA Samples

A sample is taken from each individual. It can be blood, semen, a strand of hair, or a piece of fingernail. The sample can be old or new as long as its cells contain DNA. The DNA of each person is very much like everyone else's DNA. But a few sequences are so different from person to person—in length and sequence—that they

57

can be considered a personal I.D. These I.D. sequences are called *restriction fragment length polymorphisms*. Fortunately, they're usually called *RFLPs*, for short.

RFLPs are DNA sequences of varying length that can be restricted, or marked off. The marked locations (or *loci*, the Latin plural of *locus*) must have three characteristics. They have to be different from person to person (be *polymorphic*). They must follow Mendel's inheritance laws. And they must have low mutation rates. They must also be scientifically documented, so outside experts can examine and interpret the results.

The first technique used in producing an RFLP has already been described. The cell's DNA is cut with restriction enzymes that home in on target beginning and end points called *recognition sites*. Several enzymes are used, allowing cuts at different locations.

It's as if one had two identical multicolored ribbons (see figure 14). One ribbon would be cut at the blue markers on either side of the green section. The second one would be cut at the red markers.

In the genetic process, each enzyme is designed to recognize and make a cut at a specific nucleotide base sequence, such as CCGG. For accurate comparison, several different enzymes are used on samples of an individual's DNA, each enzyme cutting at a different location.

The RFLPs differ from person to person in three ways: nucleotide *base change*, DNA segment *insertion*, and DNA segment *deletion*.

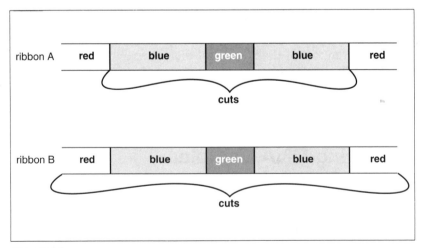

Figure 14

R F L P s

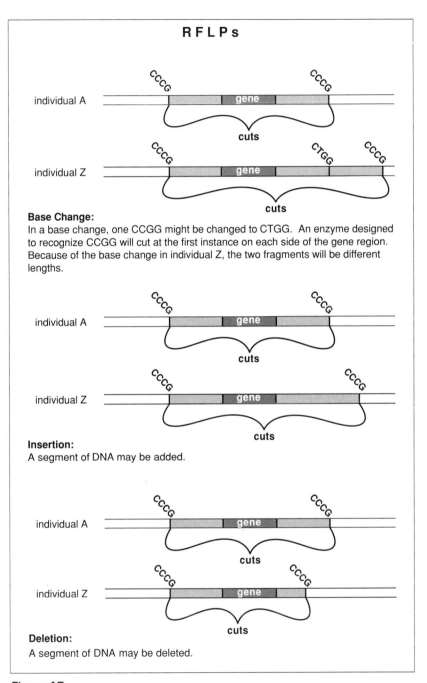

Base Change:
In a base change, one CCGG might be changed to CTGG. An enzyme designed to recognize CCGG will cut at the first instance on each side of the gene region. Because of the base change in individual Z, the two fragments will be different lengths.

Insertion:
A segment of DNA may be added.

Deletion:
A segment of DNA may be deleted.

Figure 15

RFLP Preparation

In the laboratory, the nuclear DNA is alternately dissolved in a fluid and precipitated (separated from the fluid) several times to remove structural and other cellular material, until only DNA remains in solution. The restriction enzymes are then added and the mixture is heated, activating the "digestion" process that cuts the DNA at the recognition sites. This step is known more formally as cleaving (cutting).

Next, the fragments are sorted by length in a technique called electrophoresis. In this process, the fragments are mixed with an agarose gel and an electrical current is applied. The electrically charged fragments sort by size. The gel is then washed and dried, ending up a lot like a thin sheet of gelatin dessert or fruit leather.

Finally, each subject's RFLPs are transferred from the gel to a solid support—a membrane, usually a nylon filter. This is done by making a sandwich of filter paper, the gel, a sheet of nylon filter, more filter paper, dry blotting paper, a 3-inch- thick layer of paper toweling, and a one-pound weight. After at least six hours, the fragments transfer from the gel to the membrane in what is called a *Southern transfer*. It is named for the scientist, Edwin Southern, who devised the process. The resulting membrane is called a Southern blot.

So far, the RFLPs are invisible. Now they must be made visible by adding a radioactively labeled piece of DNA called a *probe*. The process is called probe binding. Then a picture is taken of the RFLP.

This is a 373Å DNA sequencing system made by Applied Biosystems. It consists of a color printer for printing four-color "electropherograms" of sequence data; an electrophoresis unit, which houses the slab gel plates and electronics for automated electrophoresis; and a Macintosh® computer for controlling the system and viewing analyzed results.

Probe Binding

Probes work because their nucleotide sequences are designed to bind to known sequences within restriction fragments. The DNA double strands are separated, and each RFLP strand binds to a complementary probe strand, using the same rules that apply naturally—A-T and C-G. The process is called *hybridization.*

More than 1,000 probes have been identified since the first one was discovered in 1980.

The blot is incubated for 16 to 24 hours in a warm solution containing the probe.

A probe carries with it a "reporter," often a radioactive tag, such as phosphorus-32, an isotope that is widely used in biomedical research. Hybridization occurs on the membrane. One membrane is prepared for each person's RFLP.

Now X-ray film is exposed to each membrane for several days at very low temperature (−94°F), using the P-32 radiation as "light." The developed film, called an *autoradiograph* (or *autorad,* for short), shows a pattern of fragments that an expert can compare to patterns on other autorads. This is the "genetic fingerprint."

(Agricultural Research, USDA)

Athanasios Theologis, a plant molecular biologist, uses electrophoresis to separate and match nucleotide sequences of DNA fragments to determine which genes are related to plant aging.

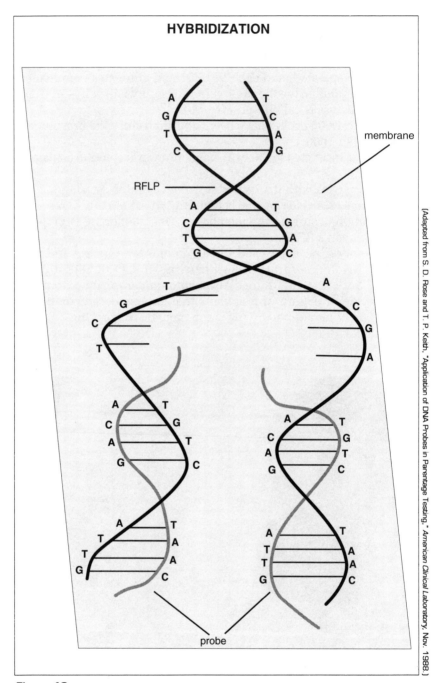

Figure 16

Comparing Patterns

Alec Jeffreys, a British scientist, developed the genetic fingerprinting technique in 1985. Its first use was in Britain to verify the parentage of an immigrant who had left the country and then wanted to return. Shortly after that, the British police used it to identify a rapist and murderer. Since that time, the technique has been perfected and is now being used in many countries.

Standard methods of operation are still in the process of being developed. But the U.S. Federal Bureau of Investigation (FBI) has set standards for its own DNA fingerprinting laboratory, and police departments around the United States are using the process.

Identifying Parents

The heart of genetic parentage testing depends on the fact that a child inherits specific genes from either one parent or the other. So the child's RFLPs should look like either the mother's or the father's. This is why it's important for the restriction fragments to be inherited according to Mendelian genetic laws and for there to be a low chance of mutation.

The child's RFLPs are compared with those of the mother and the man who may be the father. If any of the child's RFLPs fail to resemble similar RFLPs of either adult, then the man is probably not the father. This is called exclusion. If any RFLPs do resemble the man's, then he probably is the father. This is called inclusion.

While many cases involve showing whether a man is a child's genetic father when the mother is known, not all of them do. At least one famous case in Florida involved showing whether two babies were accidentally switched in the hospital years earlier and given to the wrong parents. The genetic fingerprints showed that a switch had been made. But the identification of the actual birth parents meant that the child had to rethink her own identity.

Identifying Criminals

Genetic fingerprinting is also used in law enforcement. The following scenario illustrates one possible example.

Someone has been stabbed to death. A neighbor has identified a possible suspect. And the police have good clues linking the suspect to the crime. One of them is a bloodstain on the suspect's watchband.

The question: Does the bloodstain match the victim's blood? If so, it becomes very important evidence against the suspect.

The police run two genetic fingerprints. The suspect's cell samples will come from the stain on the watchband. Samples from the victim might come from a strand of hair. In comparing Southern blots, the investigators must find RFLP matches that are exact enough to show that the stain really is the victim's blood.

The important words in the last sentence are "exact enough," because not everyone thinks that RFLP comparisons can be believed.

Is Genetic Fingerprinting Reliable?

There is one big difference between old-fashioned fingerprinting based on the pads of the fingers and genetic fingerprinting. The accuracy of genetic fingerprinting is given as a probability ratio, not a certainty.

No expert will testify that an autorad comparison actually "proves" parentage or that the bloodstain on the watchband absolutely came from the victim. Instead, the expert will say, for instance, that the chances are 1 in 100 million that the similarity in autorads is a coincidence.

One laboratory states that the use of four probes can show better than 99.99 percent probability of parentage. Using four probes can give a billion-to-one probability that two people have identical blots. Those are pretty good odds, but they're not absolute.

Scientific Arguments

Many molecular biologists support genetic fingerprinting. But some specialists are skeptical, based on several arguments:

- How confident is the expert in the results? How do you calculate the odds?
- How are the autorads interpreted? For instance, are pieces of DNA that might or might not be contaminants disregarded?
- Different experts interpret autorads differently: Sometimes electrophoresis causes changes because some fragments move faster than others.
- There aren't any worldwide standards for performing genetic fingerprinting. Different kinds of probes are used in different countries. And not everyone runs control fragments, which

have known values, along with the samples. Without controls, it's harder to tell if the electrophoresis has made a change.

- Experts make assumptions, or judgments, before determining the probability of a match. In several criminal cases, the experts began by assuming that the suspect committed the crime, then calculated the odds of a genetic fingerprint match.

- Another problem with the test is that only a few DNA locations are tested, rather than the pattern created by the hundreds of thousands of locations that actually exist.

- A major criticism involves the frequency of RFLPs in ethnic and racial groups—that is, how likely it is that two people within a group will have the same RFLP. Right now, frequencies have been calculated for Caucasians, African Americans, and Hispanics. But within each group are subgroups. In Caucasians, are the frequencies different for northern European and southern European ancestry? How about western Europe versus eastern Europe? And how about people whose ancestors came from many different places? Is there a difference in people whose ancestors came to America in the 20th century and those with ancestors who came earlier? Again, how about people whose ancestors came various times?

Scientists who support the use of genetic fingerprinting say that statistical methods have taken these differences into account. But others still disagree about the use of RFLPs.

Legal Arguments

An RFLP evaluator begins by assuming that there is as much of a chance that the suspect is guilty as that he or she is innocent. But the basic assumption of the U.S. Constitution is that someone accused of a crime is presumed innocent until proven guilty.

Older kinds of genetic tests also use statistical interpretation. In throwing out the results of one such test, the Wisconsin Supreme Court said that it goes against "our system of criminal justice to allow the state, through the use of statistical evidence which assumes that the defendant committed the crime, to prove that the defendant committed the crime." The same argument might be used against genetic fingerprinting.

Because of questions about its accuracy, genetic fingerprinting has not been accepted in all courts. Also, some courts that do accept the test require higher accuracy than others do.

Another difficulty with using genetic fingerprinting in court is that juries, made up of ordinary people unlikely to be familiar with molecular genetics, may have difficulty objectively evaluating the testimony. Some jurors tend to go along with the scientific experts, because, as one is quoted as saying, "you can't argue with science."

To get around this problem, some judges hear arguments about the admissibility of the evidence with the jury absent. But that means that the judges also must become familiar with it, if not expert.

In 1992 a federal appeals court in New York said that the strictest rules for use of genetic fingerprinting are not required, including the accuracy decision before the trial.

For many people, the biggest impact of genetic engineering is in the medical field. The next chapter will look at the genetic basis of disease.

5 MEDICAL USES OF GENETIC ENGINEERING

Most people are interested in celebrities. People like to know how they became famous, how healthy they are, and eventually, how they died. If a celebrity died violently, many people wonder how their lives might have continued if they had lived. Would they have lived for years in good health? Or did they have a disease that would have killed them sooner?

Abraham Lincoln is a good example. He was a poor boy who made it to the top. As president in the 1860s, he led the United States through the Civil War. Then he was assassinated—shot in the head—just as victory was in sight. Genetic scientists have a special interest in Lincoln because of his appearance.

Photos show him as tall, thin, with extremely long arms, legs, and fingers. In fact, fingers like his used to be called "spider fingers." To experts, he looks like he has a genetic condition called Marfan syndrome.

Today about 40,000 Americans have Marfan syndrome, which is carried on chromosome 15. (Chromosomes other than the X and Y are numbered according to size.) Scientists know that besides physical appearance, the syndrome also affects other parts of the body—shown in abnormal joints and bones, eyes, heart, and blood vessels. People with Marfan syndrome also have a higher than normal risk of sudden death from overexertion, which causes the aorta (a major artery) to burst.

Did Lincoln really have Marfan syndrome? Genetic engineering lets scientists examine the genetic makeup of people from the past, such as Lincoln—if any part of their DNA still exists. In Lincoln's case, it may. The National Museum of Health and Medicine has samples taken at the president's autopsy. They include bloodstains from the shirt cuffs of the physician who performed the autopsy, several strands of hair, and bone fragments from Lincoln's head wound. DNA eventually breaks down like other organic materials, but the time required depends on how the samples are handled, disturbed, and stored. Samples from Egyptian mummies and others thousands of years old have retained their DNA. If any of the Lincoln samples still contain DNA, chromosome 15 could be studied for mutations.

Whether this can be done may be decided more easily than whether it should be done. Ethics and politics, as well as science, are involved. At least one opponent of the plan believes it is a public relations gimmick to obtain more federal funding for genetic research. There are also possible commercial applications. Suppose someone decided to copy the cells of some famous person and sell them as souvenirs? Or suppose admirers have the cells incorporated into their own bodies! This may seem like science fiction right now, but it's a possibility for the near future.

Another question: Do the dead, even famous people, have the right to privacy? Or should their remains be available for examination or exploitation far in the future? When Lincoln died, someone remarked, "Now he belongs to the ages." But does that mean his DNA belongs to scientists?

Who makes the decision? Lincoln has no known direct descendants. Three of his children died in their youth. The fourth didn't have any children of his own. As there is no family member whose approval could be sought, the government will make the decision.

The museum appointed a committee of experts to look into the question and decide whether the samples should be used. The interest in Lincoln's genetics is more than curiosity. Medical records show the three Lincoln children who died young may have had some Marfan symptoms. And there's an even more tantalizing clue. About 30 years ago, a seven-year-old boy diagnosed with Marfan syndrome was found to be a distant relative of the president's. And the boy's family records show that others may have had Marfan syndrome too. Tracing a hereditary condition in a high-profile family might be easier than in ordinary ones, and might yield more information about the pattern of inheritance.

Though opinions differ on how much must be revealed about any public figure, in this case privacy isn't really an issue. The samples are on public display at the museum.

Finally, government museums have samples from many famous people, including several other presidents. Should these also be examined so that we can learn more about our former leaders? The present is the result of actions of people in the past. Their record

(Courtesy Dr. Kathleen Potter, Washington State University, previously published in *American Journal of Medical Genetics,* © 1990. Reprinted by permission of Wiley-Liss, a Division of John Wiley and Sons, Inc.)

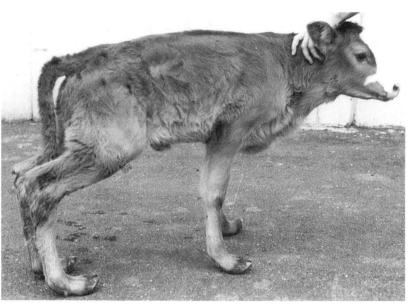

This cow has Marfan syndrome. Cows like this one are being studied to learn more about the disease.

includes laws and battles and words and pictures. Should it also include their genetic makeup?

The committee decided to approve the plan to test the Lincoln samples. But it wanted to consider how the test should be done. There's no hurry; a good test for Marfan syndrome hasn't yet been developed. And the committee of experts also wanted to be sure that the most information can be gotten from the smallest sample. Cattle with spontaneously occurring Marfan syndrome are being studied at Washington State University to test diagnostic procedures and learn more about the condition.

The Genetics of Disease

One out of every 100 babies is born with a genetic defect. The effect can be something minor or a serious problem. The problem can show up at birth or not until middle age. Besides inherited genetic problems, a person's DNA can be damaged by toxic chemicals, heat, or radiation.

At one time, scientists thought that Mendel's laws covered all inheritance. Today they know there are several kinds of inheritance. Some genetic defects are inherited following Mendel's laws. Other problems are *multifactorial*. This means they are caused by several genes or by a combination of genes and the environment. An example is Alzheimer's disease, which destroys brain cells. Genes on two different chromosomes may be involved as well as materials in the environment.

Another kind of inheritance involves mitochondria.

Mitochondrial Inheritance

The inheritance pattern of mitochondrially caused diseases is different from those caused by nuclear DNA for several reasons. A mitochondrion can have more than one copy of its DNA. Also, some cells have more mitochondria than others. Mitochondrial DNA (mtDNA) is usually inherited only from the mother, and when the cell divides, the mitochondria are assigned randomly. mtDNA mutations seem to cause a rare type of epilepsy, a type of eye paralysis, and several other diseases.

The percentage of the total mitochondria carrying a particular mutation determines whether the disease is expressed. It also determines whether it is a severe or light form. Finally, mutations occur throughout life. So a disease may not show up until later in life, when the number of mutations reaches a high enough percentage.

Two types of mitochondrial genetic mutations have been found to be related to genetic diseases. A *point mutation* is the substitution of one base for another, such as an A instead of a G. This mutation in mitochondrial DNA has been linked to a rare and inheritable form of epilepsy. A *deletion* means one or more bases are missing. In some cases, almost half of mitochondrial bases have been found missing. The deletion causes a type of eye-muscle weakness.

Inheritance, Disease, and Genetic Engineering

Today genetic engineering is being used to understand the cause of diseases and to develop possible treatments and even prevention. One of the most-studied diseases is cystic fibrosis.

Cystic Fibrosis

The lung disease called cystic fibrosis (CF) is the leading hereditary cause of death among Caucasian Americans and affects about one in 2,000—in all, 30,000 children and young adults. The disease causes a thick, sticky mucus that clogs the lungs and digestive tract and makes them vulnerable to infections, which are usually fatal. People with cystic fibrosis usually die by the age of 30. Current treatment involves pounding the body several times a day to break up the mucus and allow the person to expel it from the body.

In 1990 a group of scientists, Lap-Chee Tsui and Jack Riordan of the University of Toronto and Francis Collins of the University of Michigan, discovered the mutation that causes cystic fibrosis. The gene is on chromosome 7. The research was so precise that it identifies the exact codon that is involved for most people—a second copy of the instructions for the 508th amino acid, a phenylalanine, in the protein chain. This identification is called *sequencing*, and the fact that two genes are required to express the disease means it is recessive.

Since the gene was discovered, researchers have found about 200 different mutations. The type of mutation is probably linked with the severity of the disease.

When the gene is normal, it makes a protein that brings energy-carrying ions (electrically charged particles) into the long and digestive

Lap-Chee Tsui was one member of a group of scientists that, in 1990, discovered the mutation that causes cystic fibrosis.

71

cells, so they can work normally. This fact has been tested in cells grown in the laboratory. The next step is to create a line of laboratory animals that carry the gene, for further research on implanting normal cells in people with CF.

Other research has found that the missing protein should be on the surface of the cell. Spray medications containing the protein or the gene are being developed. To make a spray with the gene, a virus would be used as the gene carrier. Drugs to get rid of the mucus and prevent lung infections are also being developed.

Now that the cause of CF has been found, many people want to start large-scale screening tests to find who carries the gene, but this would open ethical questions.

CF Testing and Ethics

Some scientists say that people of child-bearing age or those who are pregnant should be screened for the CF gene; such a test currently exists. The idea is controversial for several reasons. First, the test works for the most common gene defect. Suppose a person takes the test and learns she or he carries the gene. What are that person's chances of passing the gene to a child? Since the CF gene is recessive, both parents would have to carry and pass the gene. The chances of carrying the gene depend on one's race. It's greatest among Caucasians. As many as one-fifth of American Caucasians carry the gene. But studies in Europe have shown that the chances are different in different parts of the continent. The chances of the disease are much less among African Americans and Asians.

The test only shows that someone is *not* carrying the most common genetic defect. It doesn't give information about the other types of CF mutations. But it does provide more information for people who want to know as much as possible about their chances of having a normal child.

Also, the test costs several hundred dollars. Many people wouldn't be able to afford it.

The CF test can also be used on unborn babies. And for people beginning in vitro fertilization—preparing the embryo in the laboratory for implantation in the mother—the egg cell can be tested for CF before the sperm is introduced. In another method, when the embryo has divided into eight cells, one cell is removed and tested for CF and several other genetic diseases. If the results are negative, the embryo can be implanted successfully. The first child who underwent this test was born in 1990.

Diabetes

Diabetes mellitus is a genetic disease in which the body can't properly use carbohydrates—sugars and starches. One in 10 Caucasian Americans have diabetes, and the rates are higher among African Americans, Mexican Americans, and Native Americans. Diabetes occurs either when cells in the pancreas called the islets of Langerhans fail to produce the normal amount of insulin or when the body does not make efficient use of the insulin that is produced. Insulin is a hormone that the body needs to maintain the blood sugar (glucose) level. If not treated, diabetes can damage the heart and blood vessels, the eyes, the nervous system, and the kidneys, and can even cause death. Insulin is also needed for cells to progress to the S phase of the cell cycle.

Diabetes brings other problems too. Women who developed diabetes as children have a two-to-three times greater risk of having babies with birth defects. These include congenital heart disease and neural tube defects, a condition in which the brain is not completely developed.

Normally, sugar is stored in the muscles and liver in the form of glycogen, which is sometimes called "muscle food." It is released and "burned" when the body performs work. Diabetics have glucose levels that are too high and abnormal glycogen storage in muscle and fat tissues.

People can develop diabetes at any age. It can't be cured, but it can be controlled. When diabetes is developed in childhood, it is called juvenile or type I. Because the person's body doesn't produce enough insulin, type I is usually controlled by injections of insulin and also regulation of sugars and other carbohydrates in the diet. Maturity or adult-onset diabetes, called type II (inefficient insulin use), affects more than 12 million people. It is usually controlled by diet along with weight reduction, if the person is overweight, and medication. Type II diabetes occurring in young people is called MODY (maturity-onset diabetes of the young).

Scientists have known for a long time that diabetes is hereditary, but its genetic origin is still being unraveled. It's probably multifactorial. Many genes (called "multiple foci") may be involved. Each one has small and additive effects, making a person more likely to develop the condition. The person is said to have *genetic susceptibility*.

Other possible factors include being overweight and the aging process. Race is also a factor. The American Diabetes Association has called diabetes among African Americans "a major chronic disease of epidemic proportions." Also, diabetic complications are more severe among African Americans.

The rate of diabetes is much higher among some Native American groups. In the Pima Indians of Arizona it is close to 100 percent. Studies show that Native Americans in many parts of the country who have kept their traditional life-styles have low rates of diabetes. Others have adopted modern diets and life-styles—higher amounts of fats and refined flour and sugar, less exercise and physical work, and more obesity. Their rate of diabetes has increased rapidly.

Mexican Americans, who as a group have about 25 percent Native American ancestry, also have a high rate of diabetes. And higher rates are also found among Native Americans in Mexico and Central America who have modern life-styles.

The same high rates of diabetes are not seen in Asia, which is the ancestral home of Native Americans. Why? Here's one theory: After the migration over the Bering Strait land bridge, living conditions changed. Perhaps there was a carbohydrate shortage. People whose bodies made more efficient use of carbohydrates had a better chance of surviving. But their descendants can't handle the larger amounts of carbohydrates in modern diets.

Diabetes is also common among Australian Aborigines and peoples of the Pacific islands.

Other environmental factors may also be involved in the development of the disease in individuals and groups.

Insulin-dependent or Juvenile (Type I) Diabetes

Type I diabetes has been found to be linked to chromosome 6 and chromosome 11. Though there's no cure for diabetes yet, it's important to predict who will become diabetic, so that a treatment program can be started as soon as possible. In 1990 scientists at the University of Texas Southwestern Medical Center at Dallas made a big step in predicting who has a good chance of developing diabetes.

They found that a region of chromosome 6 controlled dominant inheritance or dominant protection in diabetes in Caucasians. It had already been shown that this region controlled a protein called HLA, or the human leukocyte antigen. The Texas scientists' method sent *oligonucleotides* (known sequences) as probes into a chromosome 6 and observed where they landed. This is called DNA tissue typing.

The information was combined with the results of older tests that detected HLA. The new test is five times as accurate as the older test alone. It puts people in one of three groups of about equal size:

- Those who have the gene for dominant protection. They almost certainly will not develop diabetes.
- Those who have inherited the gene for dominant susceptibility. They have 5 to 10 times the normal risk of developing diabetes.
- Those who are "neither particularly protected nor particularly vulnerable."

Improvements in the test should be able to give 50-50 probability of developing diabetes. This is the same level of certainty as in identical twins. If one develops the disease, the other has a 50-50 chance of developing it.

In type I diabetes, the body's immune system is triggered against its own pancreas cells. Prevention could involve suppressing the immune system so that it doesn't work so well. Scientists are developing a drug to do this.

Non-insulin Dependent or Maturity-onset (Type II) Diabetes

Several genetic areas are being investigated, including chromosome 11, chromosome 19, and chromosome 20, for the cause of type II diabetes.

Mental Retardation

There are a number of causes and types of mental retardation—the inability of the brain to work at the "average" level of people in general. Two of the most common types have been widely studied by geneticists—the "fragile X" syndrome and Down syndrome.

"Fragile X" Syndrome

"Fragile X" syndrome is the most frequent cause of inherited mental retardation and is carried on the X chromosome. The syndrome consists of varying degrees of mental retardation and also hyperactivity. It occurs in one of 1,500 males and less frequently in females.

The syndrome is called "fragile X" because of an unexpected discovery in the laboratory. In testing cells from people with this syndrome, scientists discovered that the X chromosome always broke at a particular site because of the procedure used. This let them find the exact location of the gene involved. The living X chromosome doesn't break within the person's body.

The defect itself seems to be caused by an inactivated X chromosome. The inheritance is complicated. Ordinarily, one of a woman's two X chromosomes is inactivated. If the inactive chromosome is passed on to a child, it is normally reactivated. But the "fragile X" mutation may prevent reactivation. This mutation doesn't always cause retardation. The pattern of inheritance is different from family to family, and even within a family. But when this type of retardation occurs in males, it is apparently because of abnormal protein production at several places within the gene sequence.

Researchers used probes already known to home in near the "fragile X" point. The probes were incorporated in chromosomes grown in yeast—known as *yeast artificial chromosomes*, or *YACs*. Scientists are still looking for the mutation but believe it is not a point mutation.

Down Syndrome

Down syndrome is another type of mental retardation as well as a distinctive physical appearance caused by an extra copy of part of chromosome 21. It can be inherited from either parent, or it can result from a mutation in the person with the syndrome. About 15,000 children are born with Down syndrome each year in the United States.

Research into the cause of Down syndrome is being performed with a number of laboratory model species. *E. coli* bacteria is being used to investigate differences in protein production between normal cells and those carrying the chromosome mutation. Scientists make use of "libraries" (known sequences) of DNA or RNA cloned in various tissues, such as bird liver cells. Mouse models, whose chromosome 16 is the equivalent of human chromosome 21, are used to study the syndrome in living mammals.

Studies have shown that a child's chance of having Down syndrome increases with the age of the mother. Many pregnant women undergo screening tests to learn if their child carries the mutation. The first test uses a combination of the mother's age and a test of the mother's blood for alpha-fetoprotein (AFP). AFP is produced by the unborn child's liver and ends up in the mother's bloodstream. Its level normally increases during the second trimester of a pregnancy. If the amounts of AFP in the mother's bloodstream are very low, the fetus may be at increased risk of having Down syndrome.

According to some specialists, the age-AFP screening method is a good means of screening for incomplete development of the brain, called neural tube defects. But it allows detection of only about one-fifth of Down syndrome babies before birth. It misses between 2,000 and 3,000 unborn babies each year in the United States.

After a screening or instead of it, the parents may decide to undergo amniocentesis (analysis of the amniotic fluid that surrounds the child) for chromosome analysis. Women may also undergo chorionic villus

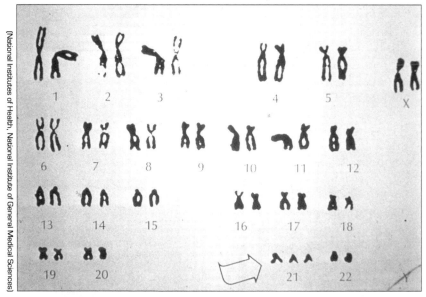

[National Institutes of Health, National Institute of General Medical Sciences]

A karyotype shows all the pairs of chromosomes in an individual arranged in numerical order, plus the sex chromosome—in both of these photos, a pair of X chromosomes. The top picture shows a normal human karyotype. The bottom picture shows the karyotype of a person with Down syndrome. Note the three chromosomes in "pair" 21.

sampling, in which tissue from a preplacental structure is analyzed for chromosomal abnormalities.

The AFP test can be made more accurate by combining it with measurements of other hormones produced by the unborn baby and the placenta.

Hemophilia

Hemophilia is an inherited disease in which the blood does not clot normally due to deficiencies or abnormalities in various blood proteins, called factors, that cause clotting. The most common deficiencies are in factor VIII and factor IX, which are controlled by the X chromosome. Other factors are controlled by autosomes.

Hemophilia affects about 20,000 people in the United States alone. It has a more public history than many other genetic disease, because the 19th-century queen Victoria of Britain was a carrier and passed it to many of her descendants. One of these was the son of the last czar of Russia. The frantic czarina, the boy's mother, turned to a mystical fanatic named Rasputin for help, which of course he could not provide. The incident was highly publicized and played a small role in the downfall of the entire Russian royal family during the Russian Revolution.

The disorder affects males almost exclusively. The abnormal gene must be present only on the X chromosome for males to have the disorder. Females must have the abnormal gene on both of the X chromosomes to have hemophilia. Because of this, hemophilia is extremely rare in females. If the abnormal gene is present on only one of a female's X chromosomes, the female is a carrier for the disorder. While a carrier does not have hemophilia, her children may inherit her abnormal gene. Hemophilia is treated with infusions of clotting factor when a bleeding episode occurs.

Large numbers of people with hemophilia who were receiving infusions of blood factors during the 1980s developed AIDS. At that time, HIV (the AIDS-causing virus) was present in the blood supply from which clotting factor was made; as a result, more than half of the people with hemophilia were infected with HIV. Since 1985 the blood supply in the United States has been screened for HIV.

The scientific community has since turned to genetic engineering to produce synthetic factor VIII that is not made from human blood, thus avoiding the AIDS virus and other contaminants. Hundreds of hemophilia patients are currently receiving this type of clotting factor on an experimental basis; its widespread use is expected soon.

Exact identification of the gene responsible for factor VIII hemophilia is difficult, because there are many mutations on the most likely gene, which is very large. Also mutations elsewhere on the X chromosome may be the cause of the disease in perhaps 40 percent of the patients.

The ultimate goal of medical genetic engineering is to treat or prevent disease at the gene level—what is called gene therapy.

Gene Therapy

The dream of transferring foreign genes into someone's abnormal cells to cure or prevent disease will become reality during the 1990s. The idea has been under development since the early 1970s. Laboratory tests with animals and some tests on humans have already pointed the way.

One of the basic techniques of gene transfer was described in an earlier chapter—inserting genetic material into a bacterium or virus, then sending it into the body. But the human body is complicated. It has many systems that provide checks and balances, or defense, against intruders or changes.

In general, there are two kinds of gene therapy. Treatment of the germ line, or reproductive cells, can be passed on to the person's children. Treatment of somatic, or body, cells benefits the individual alone. The idea of making genetic changes that can be inherited raises many objections.

The Eugenics Movement

When scientific plant and animal breeding was developed, the idea of using the same methods to create a master race or super race wasn't far behind. Just like plant improvement, the "best" humans can be bred to other "best" humans. The "worst" or the "defectives" can be weeded out.

People can be relatively objective about the "best" traits for peas, tulips, or corn. But when determining the future of other people, cultural preferences, race hatred, and other personal opinions come into play. Many nations and governments adopted ideas of "eugenic improvement" (*eugenic* comes from a Greek word meaning "well born"). In the United States, earlier in the 20th century, many people with mental illness and mental retardation were sterilized without their consent. In some places criminals were also sterilized without their consent. The most notorious policy occurred in Nazi Germany in the 1930s and 1940s, when supposedly scientific experiments were performed on adults and children who were in concentration camps. The purpose was to eliminate "inferior" ethnic groups and provide methods of purifying the German "master race."

For these reasons, any plan to improve people's health by changing their reproductive cells rings alarm bells. The same methods that improve health could also be used to change people's hair, eye, or skin color, perhaps without their knowledge or consent. It might even be possible to add genes that cause death or disease, rather than improving health.

Most scientists are more comfortable with the idea of somatic cell therapy.

Gene Therapy for Somatic Cells

Two of the biggest challenges in somatic gene therapy are that there are so many cells requiring treatment and most cells have short lifetimes. A red blood cell, for example, lives only about three months. Suppose scientists insert new genetic material to treat a disease such as sickle-cell anemia, which is a blood cell disorder carried in a gene on chromosome 11. If they treat the red cells, in a few months the cells will die, and so will the added genes.

There is a way around this problem. Stem cells are able to divide many times—they are what is called *immortal*—and they can develop into different types of cells. So if the treatment gene is inserted into a stem cell, which is then placed into the person's body, the cell would keep reproducing the new gene for life.

Some researchers have used bacteria and viruses to introduce the new gene. Other researchers have concentrated attaching the gene to a fat or protein, then injecting it directly into the body.

In the early 1990s, several gene therapies are being tried on humans. In the United States, before each stage of the project, the scientists must receive permission from the Recombinant DNA Advisory Committee of the National Institutes of Health (NIH).

Gene Therapy Experiments

The first attempt at gene therapy experimentation in the United States was in 1980. A scientist was denied permission by his university to attempt gene transplants to cure thalassemia, a blood disorder that affects people from the Mediterranean region. He then went to Italy and Israel, where he performed his experiments. (They didn't work.) After this incident, no human experiments were permitted in the United States until 1989.

In the meantime, various agricultural experiments were also waiting to be performed. The current U.S. rules for human therapy experiments were written with the safety of all genetic engineering research in mind. They permitted an experiment to treat what has been called the "bubble boy" disease.

"Bubble Boy" Disease

In the 1970s a boy named David was born with an immune system deficiency—he had no body defenses against invading germs. In an attempt to save his life, David was placed in a large plastic bubble, a self-contained environment that prevented germs from entering. He lived into his early teens but was never able to enter the world of his family and friends.

The real name of David's disease is ADA deficiency, for the name of the enzyme, adenosine deaminase, that his body couldn't make. Only a few children have the disease, which is carried on the X chromosome. The gene mutation destroys immune system cells. Today it is treated with injections of the enzyme or with transplants of bone marrow.

But there are problems with both treatments. The injections don't completely restore the immune system. And the bone marrow transplant depends on a very good match between the child's tissue and the donor's. Sometimes even close relatives don't have similar tissue.

In 1990 scientists at the NIH received permission to try gene therapy for the condition in a four-year-old girl. It was the first human gene therapy trial approved in the United States.

Copies of the normal gene for the ADA enzyme were inserted into an inactive virus. The virus was then allowed to infect some of the girl's T cells (part of the immune system). These cells were grown into a colony of 1 billion cells. Then they were put into her body like an ordinary blood transfusion. The child has returned for further transfusions.

By 1992, the treatment appeared to be successful. The engineered cells have remained at work in her system, and her immune system has grown strong. Scientists plan to use the treatment on other children who can't make use of the enzyme or bone marrow treatments.

The Future of Gene Therapy

The success of the ADA deficiency treatment is expected to lead to treatments for other genetic diseases. Laboratory tests for other diseases are in progress.

In Canada, for instance, several children have received an experimental treatment for Duchenne muscular dystrophy. This recessive disease, carried on the X chromosome, prevents production of a protein called dystrophin, which is required for normal muscle use. It is seen in babies and prevents full use and control of muscles. The children with the condition spend their lives in wheelchairs.

The Canadian test involved muscle injections of normal myoblasts—muscle cells—donated by each child's father. The myoblasts appeared to make the muscles stronger.

Scientists in Texas are developing an engineered cell that could be used in treatment of type I diabetes.

And in 1992 a test in laboratory animals of gene therapy for cystic fibrosis has been successful. A normal gene was inserted into a deactivated cold virus. Then the virus was sent into the animals' lungs. There the normal gene produced the protein that prevents buildup of the CF mucus. Human trials of the method could begin in 1993.

Genetic research and engineering methods are also adding hope for more effective treatment and prevention of many kinds of cancer. The next chapter will discuss this topic.

6 GENETICS AND CANCER

In many ways, cancer cells are like weeds. They reproduce faster than normal cells. They grow and thrive in conditions other cells can't. And eventually cancer cells overrun normal ones, destroying them if not stopped.

Normal cell cycle research and cancer research have been partners for a long time. Findings in each field help the other. The first cancer-causing gene was discovered in the late 1970s. In 1988 the first gene was found that prevents cancer. As with other genetic diseases, knowing how genes cause the disease is the first step to finding genetic treatments or prevention.

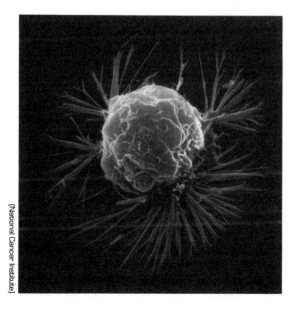

The scanning electron microscope produces a three-dimensional picture of a human breast cancer cell, showing the overall shape of the cell's structure at a very high magnification.

The Roles of Genes in Cancer Development

Cancer is an umbrella word. It includes many separate diseases involving many different kinds of cells. But the cells have several things in common. They are tremendously energetic. They grow very fast. Their shapes and sizes are different from those of normal cells. They are likely to have multiple copies of some genes—what is called *gene amplification*. And they are immortal, reproducing endlessly.

In the cell cycle, signals as well as timing start and stop the stages of growth and reproduction. The signals come from inside the cell and from the tissue the cell is part of. As a product of signals and timing, cancer too is a process, not an event.

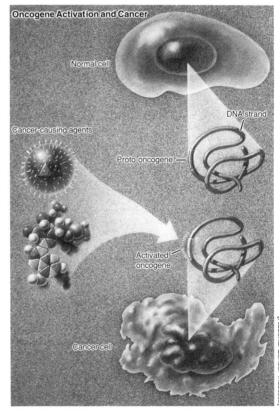

This diagram illustrates the activation of an oncogene by cancer-causing agents.

[National Cancer Institute]

Oncogenes

The genes that cause cancer are called *oncogenes*. (*Onco* means "cancer.") So far more than 60 oncogenes have been discovered. One widely studied oncogene is called *myc*. Normally myc is active in young and growing cells but inactive in older cells. But it works overtime in cancer cells, encouraging fast and uncontrolled growth. Myc has frequently been found to be amplified in cancer cells.

Tumor Suppressors

Genes that prevent cancer are called *tumor suppressors*. When they are present in the cell, they prevent cancer. When they are missing or damaged, they allow cancer to develop. In 1988 scientists at the University of California, San Diego, led by Wen-Hwa Lee, identified and cloned the first tumor suppressor—the retinoblastoma, located on chromosome 13. As the name shows, it was originally associated with a rare eye cancer in children. It is now linked to certain breast, bone and lung cancers as well.

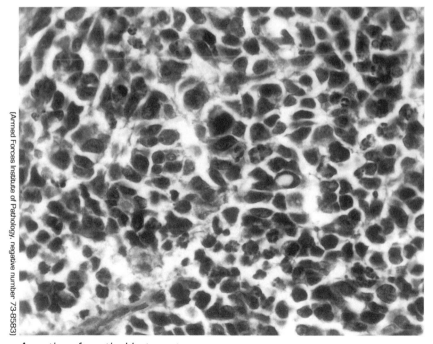

[Armed Forces Institute of Pathology, negative number 73-85583]

A section of a retinoblastoma tumor.

The second tumor suppressor discovered is called p53, located on chromosome 17. When p53 is normal, it prevents replication of DNA, keeping the cell from dividing. But when it is damaged—for instance, by toxic substances—it does two things. It permits DNA replication. And it triggers other genes that allow cancer to develop, such as oncogenes. Or it can abnormally turn on genes that produce hormones called growth factors. This lets cells grow uncontrollably. It can also trigger production of the wrong receptors on the cell surface. This allows chemicals to enter that otherwise would be kept out.

Another tumor suppressor gene discovered in 1991 is involved in colon cancer. Called M.C.C., it controls the beginning of the process from normal cell to polyp. This is the first stage in the development of the disease. The gene is located on chromosome 5.

Genetic cancer research is a new and fast-moving science. By the time this book is published, new cancer genes and new ways to detect and treat cancer will have been discovered. But most of the future discoveries will be based on today's research. Here are some of the landmarks of genetic cancer research in the early 1990s.

Bladder Cancer

Bladder cancer is very common, particularly among senior citizens. In 1990 there were 45,000 cases in the United States. In 1991 scientists at Johns Hopkins University, led by Bert Vogelstein, discovered the mutations of the p53 gene that are associated with this cancer. Several of the mutations involved a single base-pair substitution, causing an instruction for the wrong amino acid. These are called *missense* mutations. *Nonsense* mutations are those in which the gene was terminated instead of continuing with codons for amino acids. A series of amino acids also was deleted.

Identification of the exact mutated codons involved several laboratory techniques. The first was *polymerase chain reaction*, or *PCR*, which amplified (made many copies) of several p53 exons. These were then inserted into a *bacteriophage*, which is a virus that attacks bacteria, and cloned. The clones were combined with radioactive probes, which were sent into p53 genes.

In bladder cancer, some cells are washed out of the body in urine, allowing the research method's use to test urine samples of people with a high risk of the disease. The test could also be used for people who have already been treated for bladder cancer, to see if it has recurred.

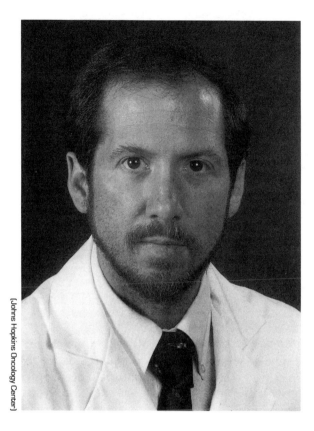

In 1991 Bert Vogelstein led the group of Johns Hopkins University scientists that discovered the mutations of the p53 gene associated with bladder cancer.

Similar tests could be used for lung, colon, and cervical cancers, whose cells also wash out of the body.

Li-Fraumeni Syndrome

For many scientists, research on a single kind of cancer is a life's work. Li-Fraumeni syndrome is the very high risk of young members of some families for a range of cancers, including breast, brain, bone, and leukemia as well as others. It is named for the two National Cancer Institute researchers who defined it in 1969, Frederick Li and Joseph Fraumeni. It wasn't until 1990 that researchers, including Li and Fraumeni, discovered how the syndrome worked.

The syndrome involves a p53 mutation for a single codon. Simply, family members who don't have the mutation don't have the syndrome's cancers. The mutation was found in both cancer and normal cells, meaning it was inherited. But because someone with the mutation has only one or a few of the cancers, a series of mutations may be needed to complete the cancer process.

Testing for the Syndrome

Li, Fraumeni, and their colleagues have begun a study of 100 families with the syndrome. All the members of each family will be tested, those with cancer and those without it. By identifying carriers of the gene as well, the pattern of inheritance is expected to show why the types of cancer are different in various family members. And it may also show why the frequency of cancer types is different than in the general public. For instance, in the general population, about the same numbers of breast and colon cancers occur. But in the Li-Fraumeni families, there are many more breast cancers.

What Do Genetic Tests Mean for Society?

The ability to develop genetic tests for people's risk of developing cancer—or other genetic diseases—raises several questions for the public to consider. In a way, these tests are part of the eugenics problem already discussed. Suppose a woman has a test and learns

[National Cancer Institute]

National Cancer Institute scientists Frederick Li (left) and Joseph Fraumeni defined Li-Fraumeni syndrome in 1969 and then worked with others to discover how the syndrome operated.

that her p53 gene has mutations that could cause cancer. Who should know about it? That person and her family? Certainly. But how about her health insurance company? Suppose the company decides it doesn't want to insure her for cancer. How about her employer? Or her landlord? If they decided they didn't want to give her a job or rent her an apartment, is that discrimination?

This issue has been raised in several states already. In 1991 in California, for instance, the state legislature passed a bill preventing job and rental discrimination and also requiring insurance companies to pay for genetic screening tests. The governor vetoed the bill because he thought it was too early to make decisions about testing in the field of genetics. Also, he didn't want to make any changes in the existing fair-housing laws. As more genetic tests are developed and used, more people will be touched by them.

Gene Therapy for Cancer

The so-called war on cancer has been going on for decades, yet the cancer rate has not gone down. Scientists have urged people to change their life-styles to lower their chances of developing cancer—giving up smoking, eating fewer fats, and avoiding toxic chemicals at work and in the environment. Treatment of cancer involves surgery and therapy with radiation and chemicals—refinements of old medical procedures.

Medical science is just beginning a new way of treating cancer—with genetic materials and techniques. Plans are even being made to use cancer cells themselves—inactivated, of course—to stop cancer from spreading in the body. Some cancer cells stay where they are. They just pile up on top of each other. Others move out from the original location, to a new location or even a new organ of the body, and start growing. Many of them have a bag of tricks they can use on cells in the new location, such as mimicking immune system cells or turning other cells' genes on or off. By taking advantage of some of these "skills," scientists may be able to turn cancer cells into vectors for engineered genes.

One of the biggest fears, even among scientists, is that gene therapy could cause cancer, even while it is trying to treat it. The ability to deliver genetic material to a precise location in the target cell's DNA is vital for success without the risk of cancer. Delivery to the wrong location could trigger other genes that start or speed up the cancer process.

In 1992 the most promising therapy—for a form of skin cancer called melanoma—is undergoing human tests at the National Institutes of Health.

Melanoma Therapy

Melanoma is a highly lethal type of skin cancer, with a death rate of over 80 percent. Conventional treatments don't always work, especially if treatment doesn't begin early. In 1989 scientists at the NIH received permission to use cells called tumor infiltrating lymphocytes (TILs) on people who were dying of melanoma. TILs are known to attack tumors and destroy them. The NIH test wasn't meant to be a treatment, but rather a first step to see if the TILs reached the target tumor. The cells were tagged with special genes that scientists could follow to the destination.

This test was successful, so the next step was to use TILs as a test treatment on other patients. A gene that controls production of a protein called tumor necrosis factor, which destroys tumors, was inserted into the TILs' DNA. The altered TILs were then injected into the patients as a blood transfusion. The main problem was to provide

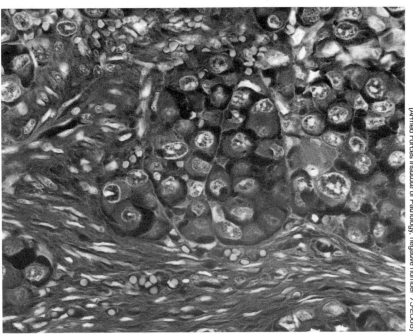

Malignant melanoma

[Armed Forces Institute of Pathology, negative number 75-2068]

enough tumor necrosis factor to destroy a tumor without damaging normal surrounding cells or upsetting other body functions. The test treatment was carried out in 1991. It worked well enough to make tumors shrink or disappear in several patients. Several others died, however.

7 GENES IN RESEARCH AND BUSINESS

The first world maps were made in the 1500s. Depicting the coastlines of the continents and islands, they showed the major landmarks. Mapmakers added features and distances as they studied regions more closely. Today a different kind of mapping is also underway—a map of all the 50,000 to 100,000 genes (2,000 now identified) in the human body, what is called the human *genome* (**gen**e + chromos**ome**). It involves over 3 billion base pairs. In the nucleus of one human cell, the DNA coils tightly into 23 pairs of chromosomes. Uncoiled it would stretch six feet long.

Just as maps of the earth show landmarks and the distances between them, a genome map would show gene locations and distances between them as well as every "rung" on the DNA "ladder" (every base pair). This knowledge would be the basis for:

- better health—identifying the location of specific disease genes so people could be tested for these genes and then make life-style changes or, in the future, receive gene or other therapy that might prevent the disease.
- understanding of evolution—helping to learn how life originated on earth or elsewhere in the universe and how the human species (and others) evolved.
- basic science information—the genome is one of the great unknowns of the way the human body works.

Right now, human genome maps are like old maps of North America—they have a few landmarks and lots of unknown "deserts." In other words, the scientists know some of the base sequences, but there are still many gaps. The same is true of genome maps of other species. Only those of some viruses are complete. But by the year 2010, a precise map of the entire human genome may be available—including the name and position of every base pair in human DNA.

Discovering the name—A, G, T, or C—of each base in the 3 billion base pairs is such a huge job that no one scientist or country can do it alone. Scientists in the United States, Japan, the European Community, and many other places have divided up the project and are working on different parts of the genome map at the same time. In the United States, several chromosomes are being mapped—chromosome 4 at the University of California, San Francisco; chromosome 7 and the X chromosome at Washington University, St. Louis; and chromosome 11 at the Salk Institute in San Diego.

The worldwide project will cost many billions of dollars. It is being coordinated by the Human Genome Organization, known as HUGO.

In the United States, two federal agencies are the major partners—the National Institutes of Health and the Department of Energy. The NIH is concentrating on genes related to disease. The Department of Energy is constructing maps and developing methods of actually determining the DNA sequences.

Along with the human genome, the genomes of other species are being mapped too. Some of them are important for medical research.

The fruit fly genome is important for genetics studies. The cacoa (or chocolate) genome is one of many that are being studied for their use in agriculture. Zoologists are mapping the genomes of endangered animals, and plant biologists are doing the same for endangered plants.

Although exciting, the human genome project is also controversial as well as large and costly. Many of the most famous people in genetic reasearch support the project. In fact, James Watson was the first head of the NIH's genome project. Supporters say the the complete human genome is needed because it's the best way to use research dollars to improve human health. They also think that a big, coordinated project will avoid duplication of effort. Without it, scientists might be mapping the same chromosomes while neglecting others.

But other distinguished scientists don't favor it. A big project will take money needed for other medical work. Some scientists say that health dollars will do more good if they are spent on better health care before birth, than to prevent birth defects by genetic means.

Part of the argument also depends on one's point of view. People with genetic diseases may want research to concentrate immediately on the causes and cures. Some research scientists may be willing to wait a longer time for useful information—until the whole project is completed.

Geneticists began looking at the composition of genes even before DNA's double helix was discovered. The real effort to discover the genome's exact composition began in the 1970s. It wasn't until 1986 that the international program was organized. The genome project involves two main activities—mapping and sequencing.

Mapping the Genome

Like geographic maps, there are different kinds of genome maps. And each kind has different levels of detail. The two main types of genome maps are *genetic* and *physical*.

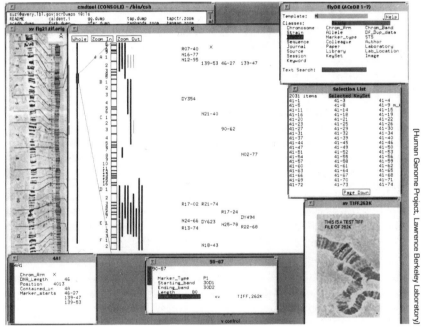

(Human Genome Project, Lawrence Berkeley Laboratory)

The above picture and the picture on page 95 show images from computers employed by the Human Genome Project. This image presents information on *Drosophila* DNA. The photolike image on the left shows a piece of DNA; to its immediate right is a map of that DNA. The photolike image on the bottom right is what is seen under the microscope—the computer converts this to the straightened-out image that is mapped above. *The image on page 95 is an autoradiogram physical map of human chromosome 21. Each line represents the fingerprint of a DNA clone. Examiners compare the lines. The graph at the bottom left shows the intensity of the various lines.*

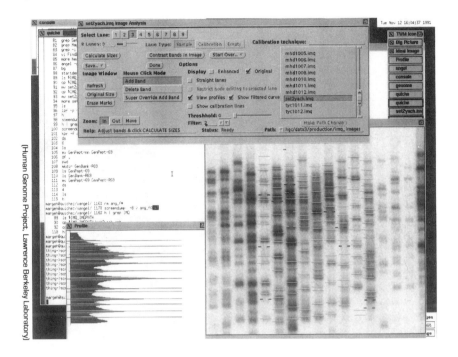

Genetic Maps

Genetic maps have another name—linkage maps. These were the kind of maps Morgan used in his *Drosophila* laboratory. Linkage maps have been brought into the genetic engineering era to locate relative positions of genes or of gene markers, such as RFLPs. Distances on the linkage map show how likely two genes are to recombine during meiosis. The farther apart they are, the more likely they are to recombine. In honor of Morgan, the distances are measured in centimorgans (cM). Scientists believe that one cM equals about 1 million base pairs.

A linkage map based on several generations of a family, for instance, can reveal gene positions, even if the physical position isn't known. Or it can be used to check the accuracy of a physical position. Today's detailed linkage maps show distances of only 3 to 5 cM.

Physical Maps

Physical maps show the actual distances between genes, measured in numbers of base pairs separating them. The final human genome map will be physical, showing the exact name and location of each base pair.

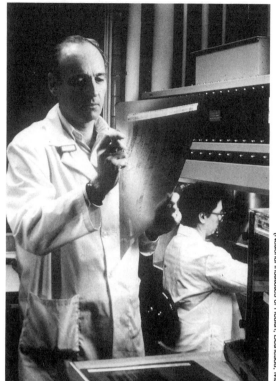

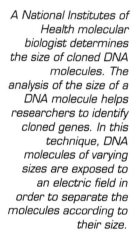

A National Institutes of Health molecular biologist determines the size of cloned DNA molecules. The analysis of the size of a DNA molecule helps researchers to identify cloned genes. In this technique, DNA molecules of varying sizes are exposed to an electric field in order to separate the molecules according to their size.

(National Institutes of Health, Bethesda, MD)

Two kinds of physical maps are being made at the same time. A *macrorestriction map* shows a set of large DNA fragments found through the RFLP technique. RFLPs containing a rare sequence make their DNA cuts very far apart, producing a large ("macro") fragment. This kind of map is a good early step in understanding the makeup of a larger section of DNA, such as a chromosome.

An *ordered clone map* arranges the relative positions of fragments cloned in YACs, viruses, or plasmids. Pairs of clones can be compared using the genetic fingerprinting method to show if there is any overlap (if they are *contigs*, meaning contiguous). Or they can be hybridized, then compared.

Connecting Linkage and Physical Maps

The two kinds of maps have something in common—they're based on landmarks. A technique called *sequence tagged site (STS)* mapping lets scientists use the same landmarks on both maps. These landmarks are unique identifying sequences for each gene or probe. Using STSs depends on a technique called *polymerase chain reaction* (*PCR*) for quickly making copies of an STS fragment.

PCR is based on the natural processes of transcription, translation, and DNA repair. DNA strands are heated to break the connecting chemical bonds, the "rungs." Then artificial ends of the wanted sequence, called *primers*, are placed in the middle. An enzyme adds the complementary bases between the artificial ends and restores the bonds, creating two double strands where only one had been. The process allows fast production of billions of STS fragment copies.

The "language" of STS fragments is the pairs of primers that define each fragment.

Sequencing

The genome maps now being made will be a guide to *sequencing*— finding the exact name and position of each base pair. Sequencing is done using several techniques already described, including gel electrophoresis and blots. Scientists are developing ways to perform these techniques faster and cheaper. New methods are also expected to speed the process:

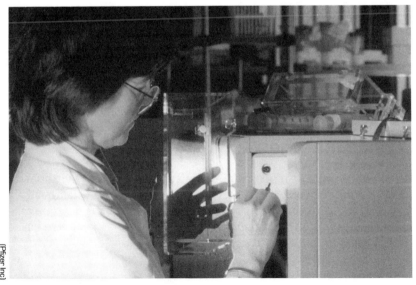

[Pfizer Inc]

Automated DNA sequencing analysis has improved scientists' ability to search for genes implicated in disease at a dramatically increasing rate.

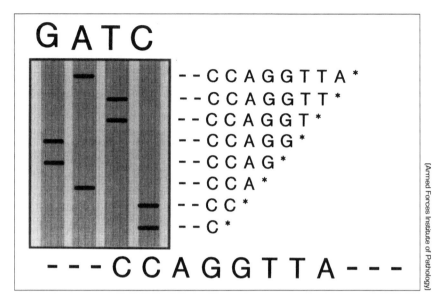

This image correlates the stripes in an autoradiogram to a sequence of bases.

- *Hybridization* uses a combination of short sequences detected by probes and computer algorithms (math routines) to assemble long sequences.
- *Flow cytometry* assigns a different label to each base. When a sequence is released one base at a time, each one is identified by its label.
- *Scanning tunneling microscopy* examines each base, one atom at a time. A different label on each base allows identification of the members of a sequence.

Other Genomes

Identification of the genomes of other species is being coordinated with the human project. The first priority for research scientists has been organisms useful in studying human genetics. The genome of a nematode (roundworm), *Caenorhabditis elegans*, has been used as a pilot project for other species. *C. elegans* is widely used for studies of the nervous system. Brewer's yeast, *Saccharomyces cerevisiae*, is used for cell-cycle studies. It is being mapped at Stanford University. Genomes of *Mycoplasma capricolum*, a wall-less bacterium, and *Escherichia coli*, a bacterium of the intestinal tract, are also being mapped. *E. coli* is being used to study mitochondria as well as in biological research in general. The mouse genome, being mapped at the Massachusetts Institute of Technology, is important because mice are used as living models for disease research.

Drosophila continues to be important for genetic studies, including embryo development. It is also used for investigation of a set of genes called the *homeobox*, which is found unchanged in a wide range of organisms, including humans. This research is providing information about how evolution occurs.

For plant studies, the genome of the simple weed *Arabidopsis thaliana* is being mapped.

Other genome research is underway also—commercial research that can be used to improve agricultural products or produce new drugs and chemicals. All of it is expensive, and some of it is expected to provide large profits for the manufacturers. Genome economics has led to something that no one would have thought of a generation ago—the patenting of living organisms.

Patenting Living Things

When the U.S. government began over 200 years ago, one of the first agencies set up was the Patent and Trademark Office. A trademark is a name or symbol for a specific product. A patent applies to an invention. The steamboat and sewing machine were patented. So are computer chips and video players. Living things are part of the patent system too. For instance, some vegetables come from patented seeds.

Anything someone invents, or anything natural that someone makes important changes in, can be patented—if the inventor can show that his or her method hasn't been used before. A patent is a license to protect an invention so no one can copy it without the inventor's permission. The inventor can give someone a license to copy the invention or can charge a fee for its use. Or the inventor can keep it secret so no one else can use it. But mainly the patenting system encourages inventions and their commercial use. If someone invents a product that people want to buy, no one else can imitate it and take the profits that the first person earned by being creative. A patent gives the inventor a head start, until the patent runs out in 17 years.

In the age of genetic engineering, most organisms can be patented. Few people have concerns about patented crops. An early patented life form was a bacteria species that eats up spilled oil. But the closer patents come to humans and their bodies, the more uncomfortable some people are with the idea of patenting life.

Patenting Crops

For the patent system to work, both the developer and the user must benefit. In the 1970s Congress passed a law allowing the patenting of seed crops. For example, corn farmers often buy a patented seed. It may cost more than an unpatented seed, but the farmers may get a better yield—more crop per acre. If the price for corn is high at the end of the growing season, the extra profit will make up for the higher cost of the seed. The farmer may decide to purchase patented seed again next year.

Crops may be patented because they are resistant to diseases and pests. The developers of genetically engineered plants obtain patents because of the commercial advantage to their customers and to themselves.

The patenting of crops has a down side as well as advantages. It can reduce the diversity of agriculture. At one time, many varieties of a crop were grown. Each region had its own. Today only a few varieties are grown. The varieties can be vulnerable to a disease or a pest species. In addition the genes—and advantages—of the varieties that are no longer grown are lost. In some cases, these are qualities that future farmers or consumers may want.

Genetic engineering may provide modern varieties with characteristics of the older ones. Or it may allow preservation of the older varieties themselves in DNA collections.

Patenting Genetically Engineered Organisms

In the 1980s the U.S. Supreme Court allowed changes in the genetic code of microorganisms to be patented. In 1988 the first mammal was patented. It was a strain of mice that carry a human cancer gene. The so-called Harvard mouse is one of the living models scientists use to study human disease. The Patent Office called the Harvard mouse a "composition of matter" and the product of human invention.

Animal rights groups and religious organizations objected. Higher animals are more than a composition of matter, they said, and have purposes other than to serve human needs.

Farmers' groups and others objected on economic grounds. Suppose all livestock were patented. Large companies might be able to control

Dr. Philip Leder, professor and chairman of genetics at Harvard Medical School, shows a photo of the genetically altered mouse that Harvard patented in 1988.

livestock production. Currently the owners of female animals pay a stud fee for mating or for the purchase of semen. The farmer owns the offspring. But under the patent system, the patent holder would own the offspring and could require farmers to pay royalties.

Other opponents say patenting animals is a get-rich-quick scheme that will only cost consumers more money.

Supporters of the patent system say it would bring the same benefits to animal farmers as it already does to grain and other vegetable farmers. Many people support patenting animals, saying the fears will die down when people become accustomed to the idea. That is what happened when genetically engineered plants and bacteria were first used.

The Patent Office has established procedures for the deposit of samples of patented organisms as well as the method used to produce and preserve them. In the United States, the American Type Culture Collection—which is part of an international system— holds animal embryos, bacteria, bacteriophages, cell lines, cloned genes, yeasts, oncogenes, and other DNA materials.

Patenting DNA Materials

Can DNA itself be patented? The question may seem surprising, but to researchers and developers, it seems logical to do. One of the ways DNA segments are preserved are as *cDNA*, or complementary

DNA. Making cDNA is another adaptation of the transcription process called *reverse transcription*. Messinger RNA (mRNA), which contains only the exons, is used to make its complementary DNA. This intron-free segment of DNA is then retained for research or commercial use.

Businesses have held patents on cDNA for several years. But in 1991 the National Institutes of Health (NIH) also decided to patent cDNA it had been working with. The idea of patenting research materials raised many objections as well as questions.

Scientific research is based on the free exchange of ideas. The international human genome project is an example. But some plant genomes are already part of commercial development. For example, in the United States the tomato genome is such a hot commercial property that there are two rival mapping organizations. They don't exchange information. There are three or more corn genome projects, for the same reason. The same thing is happening in other countries. In Japan, the rice genome map is secret.

U.S. patent law doesn't recognize a difference between commercial and nonprofit research. All the patent applicant must show is that the product is useful, new, and not obviously based on previous work.

Are there reasons why research shouldn't be patented? Researchers say that patents go against scientific ethics; some even say that the idea is immoral. Secrecy impedes research, according to others. And some say that the basis of any of today's research should be open to experts in the field.

But as one expert has asked, at what point in research is the right time to receive a patent? When a small segment of DNA has been isolated and saved as cDNA? A large segment? When the gene has been identified and expressed? When the protein has been identified? When a commercial use has been identified?

The NIH says that the purpose of its patent application is to protect the public's investment in research. A patent will let NIH license its research to commercial firms—what is called technology transfer.

Commercial Biotechnology

The biotechnology industry makes commercial use of genome mapping and agricultural and medical research—all work relating to the cell cycle and DNA. During the 1980s hundreds of small companies were born, and most of the major chemical and pharmaceutical companies also became involved. Today, their products are worth $150 billion a year worldwide, and about $50 billion in the United States.

The first genetic engineering technique widely used in industry was production of the *monoclonal antibody*. This process involves production of hybrid cells called *hybridomas*. Part of a hybridoma is an immune system B lymphocyte—a white cell that produces antibodies (chemicals that fight foreign bacteria and chemicals). The other part of a hybridoma is a tumor cell that can reproduce endlessly. The dangerous parts of the tumor cell are discarded.

The antibody portion of the hybridoma is prepared by immunizing a mouse with a foreign substance, or antigen, so that its B lymphocyte cells produce antibodies against the antigen. The mouse's spleen is then removed and cut into extremely small pieces to release the B cells. Myeloma (tumor) cells are removed from other mice and allowed to divide in the laboratory.

The two kinds of cells are mixed and fused. Then they are grown in a specific medium so that only those with the desired characteristics—antibody production and endless reproduction—survive. The hybridomas are then cloned to make large quantities available for use.

Hybridomas are the basis for drugs and vaccines, as are the other major genetic engineering techniques. The U.S. FDA has already approved at least 15 products for human use, and more are awaiting approval. Other products for nonhuman use also exist.

Some of these products are based on research within the companies themselves. Others are the result of cooperation among government, university, and other nonprofit research organizations—technology transfer.

An example of this cooperation occurred in 1991 with a cancer drug called taxol. Research scientists discovered taxol when they examined the bark of a tree called the Pacific yew. Several problems arose in producing the drug. Tremendous amounts of tree material are needed to make a small amount of the drug. Because the tree is very rare, there are environmental considerations about preservation of the species and its habitat. Further investigation showed that some Pacific yews were being cut during logging of other species but not being utilized. These "waste" yews could be the raw material for the drug, which a large pharmaceutical company will now make. The company has agreed to help pay for yew tree conservation.

In the meantime, a biotechnology company has developed a method of cloning yew tree cells. In the future, taxol may be made through genetic engineering, which would further protect the tree in its natural environment.

What Does Genetic Engineering Mean for the Future?

In a fast-moving field like genetic engineering, it's hard to predict what may occur in the next few years. Research is already providing interesting questions: Why does there seem to be active DNA on cell surfaces? Why do mussels seem to inherit mitochondria from both parents? Do brain cells receive their instructions from their genes or from neighboring cells? The answers to these and other questions may well shape genetic engineering in the future.

One thing is certain: Genetic engineering will change people's relationships with nature, medicine, and perhaps, as in the case of genetic testing, their own cultural values.

Several scientists have made predictions for the year 2020: People will have new definitions of health and illness. The completion of genome mapping will allow a health plan for each person, preventing genetic disease and promoting a better life. Cancer and heart disease will be prevented and cured with gene therapy. Joseph L. Goldstein, a Nobel Prize winner at the University of Texas Southwestern Medical Center, notes that 30 years ago, no one would have predicted monoclonal antibodies, genome mapping, or transgenic animals. His prediction? Expect the unexpected!

GLOSSARY

Adenine (A) A nucleic acid purine.

Amplification Natural or engineered process of making multiple copies of a gene or DNA sequence.

ATP (adenosine triphosphate) Cell organelle that stores energy produced by mitochondria, which is released by enzymes called ATPases.

Autorad Autoradiograph, similar to an X-ray picture. It is the final step in making a genetic fingerprint visible.

Bacteria One-celled organisms that can easily enter other, more complex organisms. Bacteria or their DNA are often used in genetic engineering.

Bacteriophage A virus that enters bacteria. Bacteriophages are used in genetic engineering to carry altered DNA.

Base One component of nucleic acids. There are four bases each in DNA and RNA: the purines, adenine and guanine, and the pyrimidines, cytosine and either thymine (in DNA), or uracil (in RNA).

Base pair The "rung" of a DNA double helix, made of one base from each strand, joined in the middle by a chemical bond.

Cell The smallest form of independent living matter. A cell may be an organism, like a bacterium, or it can be part of a tissue or organ in a multicelled body. Simple cells, without nuclei, are prokaryotes. Cells with nuclei are eukaryotes.

Cell cycle Cell sequence consisting of growth, reproduction (splitting), and death.

Cell differentiation The specializing of a cell into its mature form for a particular organ or function.

Cell membrane or **wall** Three-layer cell covering: a wall in plants, a membrane in other organisms.

Centimorgan (cM) Unit of measurement in a linkage map. It is named in honor of geneticist Thomas Hunt Morgan.

Chromatin Part of a cell nucleus made up of DNA and its supporting protein structure. In humans, chromatin is organized into 23 pairs of chromosomes. Depending on the stage of the cell cycle, chromatin is either condensed heterochromatin or loose euchromatin.

Chromosome A structure that supports part of a cell's DNA in higher organisms. Humans have 23 pairs of chromosomes.

Clone To make an exact copy, such as making a copy of a cell.

Codon Series of three consecutive nucleotides that contains the instructions for a single amino acid. A codon is also called a triplet.

Complementary DNA (cDNA) DNA made through reverse transcription.

Crossing over An exchange of genetic material by a pair of chromosomes during cell reproduction.

Cyclin Type of cell cycle protein that, combined with a kinase, starts and stops various stages in the cell cycle.

Cytoplasm The part of a cell that surrounds the nucleus, consisting of a gel-like or colloidal medium, flexible structural materials, and many organelles, including those that produce proteins and energy.

Cytosine (C) A nucleic acid pyrimidine.

Cytoskeleton A mesh of interacting and flexible fibers that supports cytoplasm organelles. The fiber types are microtubules, microfilaments, and intermediary filaments.

Deletion Natural or engineered removal or absence of a DNA sequence.

DNA (deoxyribonucleic acid) Chemical molecule made up of base pairs that contain genetic instructions. Each cell of each living organism contains DNA.

DNA fingerprinting Also known as typing; method of identifying an individual from unique DNA sequences.

DNA ligase An enzyme that pastes a segment of DNA into place.

Dominance, law of Genetics rule written by Gregor Mendel stating that some hereditary units (genes) are dominant over their opposites but don't modify (change) them.

Double helix The shape of a DNA molecule, like a spiral staircase.

Endoplasmic reticulum Cytoplasm membrane that holds ribosomes.

Euchromatin Loose chromatin.

Eukaryote A complex cell, like those in the human body. It is composed of an enclosed nucleus surrounded by cytoplasm. The nucleus contains chromosomes and the cytoplasm contains many organelles that perform cell activities.

Evolution, theory of Scientific theory that living beings today developed from the first living organisms billions of years ago. The theory was developed in the 19th century by Charles Darwin and others and is accepted by almost all scientists today. The theory is closely tied to the study of genetics.

Exon RNA sequences that carry protein instructions.

Flow cytometry Method of DNA sequencing that identifies the different labels attached to each of the four bases.

Gene A cell's unit of instructions for the production of a protein. A gene is a series of DNA base pairs and controls its organism's traits or characteristics.

Gene splicing The cutting out of a gene from one cell and pasting it into place in another cell's genetic material.

Genetic code The arrangement of nucleotides in triplets, or codons, each specifying a single amino acid.

Genetic engineering The use or manipulation of an individual's genetic material in order to produce desired characteristics or results in the same individual, other individuals of the same species, or other species.

Genetic susceptibility The sum of many small genetic factors that make a person more likely to inherit a genetic disease.

Genome (gene + chromo**some)** The entire DNA of a species.

Genome map The writing out of an entire chromosome, DNA sequence, or genome. For genome mapping, the two main types of map are linkage and physical.

Golgi bodies Also known as Golgi apparatus; cytoplasm membranes whose enzymes tag proteins with their destination addresses.

Growth factors Proteins that control a cell's growth.

Guanine (G) A nucleic acid purine.

Helix A spiral shape. DNA and RNA molecules are helix-shaped. A DNA helix has two strands (a double helix). An RNA helix has one strand.

Heterochromatin Condensed chromatin.

Heterozygote Organism containing both of a pair of traits, such as tall-short, though only one of them is expressed. Also called a hybrid.

Homeobox Set of genes that is found unchanged in a wide range of species. It is being studied to understand the way evolution works.

Homozygote Organism containing two copies of one of a pair of traits.

Hybrid Organism containing both of a pair of traits, such as tall-short, though only one of them is expressed. An organism like this is also called a heterozygote. Hybrid also means a genetically engineered cell with parts from different types or species.

Hybridization The binding of a probe to its complementary DNA sequence.

Hybridoma A hybrid cell made of the antibody-producing part of an immune system B lymphocyte and the immortal quality of a tumor cell. It is used as the basis for monoclonal antibodies.

Immortal Description of a cell that reproduces endlessly, such as a stem cell or a cancer cell.

Independent assortment, law of Genetics rule written by Gregor Mendel to describe the expression of several different traits at the same time. This law was later shown to be true for only some traits, not all of them.

Insertion Natural or engineered addition of a DNA sequence.

Intermediary filament Medium-size cytoskeleton fiber.

Intron RNA sequence that doesn't carry protein instructions. Its purpose is not yet known.

Isotope A variation of an element with a specified number of neutrons. Phosphorus-32, for example, has 15 protons and 17 neutrons, while phosphorus-33 has 15 protons and 18 neutrons. Some isotopes, such as phosphorus-32, are radioactive.

Kinase Type of cell-cycle protein that, combined with a cyclin, starts and stops various stages of the cell cycle.

Law of dominance See *dominance, law of.*

Law of independent assortment See *independent assortment, law of.*

Law of segregation (or **separation**) See *segregation, law of.*

Linkage Two traits or genes that are usually inherited together, unless they are separated during cell reproduction in a process of crossing over.

Linkage map A diagram that shows how likely two traits are to be inherited together. The likelihood is measured in centimorgans (cM).

Loci Locations of DNA sequences found by RFLPs.

Lysosome Cell organelle whose enzymes break down large proteins entering the cell.

Macrorestriction map A physical map that shows a set of large DNA fragments found through the RFLP technique.

Meiosis The splitting of an egg or sperm cell, so that when the two unite, the resulting cell has one set of chromosomes.

Mendelian inheritance Inheritance that follows Mendel's laws of segregation and dominance.

Messenger RNA (mRNA) RNA instructions copied from nuclear DNA and used to make proteins in the cytoplasm.

Microfilaments Large cytoskeleton fibers that allow a cell to contract or change shape.

Microtubules Large cytoskeleton fibers made of protein polymers.

Missense mutation A gene mutation that causes production of the wrong protein.

Mitochondrial DNA (mtDNA) DNA found in mitochondria.

Mitochondrion Semiindependent cell organelle that contains its own DNA. In the cell, mitochondria make energy that is stored by ATP. Mitochondria may be descended from independent prokaryotic bacteria.

Mitosis The splitting of a cell into two identical daughter cells during the M phase of the cell cycle.

Molecular biology The study of biology at the molecular level, involving RNA, DNA, and proteins.

Monoclonal antibody Genetic engineering technique in which hybridomas (cell hybrids) are cloned many times. The technique is used in pharmaceutical manufacturing.

Multifactorial A genetic change caused by several genes or by a combination of genetic and environmental factors.

Mutation A change in a gene caused by exposure to toxic chemicals, heat, or radiation; by mistakes during duplication for cell division; or by the aging process.

Non-Mendelian inheritance Inheritance that doesn't follow Mendel's laws, because it involves several genes or mitochondrial DNA or both environmental and genetic factors.

Nonsense mutation A gene mutation that ends the gene rather than continuing with the sequence of base pairs.

Nuclear matrix The supporting structure of a cell nucleus.

Nuclear transplantation Taking the nucleus of one embryo cell and transplanting it into another embryo cell.

Nucleoli Round bodies in a cell's nucleus, made of RNA and protein.

Nucleotide A subunit of DNA or RNA composed of a phosphoric acid, a sugar, and a base.

Nucleus The center of a eukaryotic cell, containing the chromosomes. It is surrounded by a double membrane filled with pores.

Oligonucleotide A sequence of nucleotides used as a probe.

Oncogene A gene that causes cancer.

Ordered clone map A physical map that arranges the relative positions of DNA segments cloned in YACs, viruses, or plasmids.

Organelle Specialized cell bodies, such as ATP, mitochondria, ribosomes, Golgi bodies, and lysosomes.

PCR (polymerase chain reaction) Method of making many copies of a DNA sequence.

Physical map A genome map that lists all the base pairs. Types of physical maps include macrorestriction and ordered clone.

Plasmid A bacteria's DNA.

Plastid An algaelike organelle in plant cells that performs photosynthesis.

Point mutation A genetic change involving a single base pair.

Polymorphism Something that has many different forms, such as the DNA sequences used as individual I.D.s.

Primer Artificial end of a DNA sequence.

Probe A piece of DNA that is complementary to a specific DNA sequence and binds with it. A probe is labeled with a radioactive isotope or other reporter (marker), so that when it finds its target it can be identified.

Prokaryote A simple cell without a nucleus. It is the structure of some types of bacteria.

Purine A type of nucleic acid base, either adenine or guanine.

Pyrimidine A type of nucleic acid base, either cytosine or thymine (in DNA) or uracil (in RNA).

Receptor Cell proteins that attract and bind specific molecules and sometimes pass them into the cell.

Recognition site The beginning or ending point of an RFLP.

Recombinant Recombined. In genetic engineering, it means a piece of DNA that has a section from another cell or organism.

Regulator gene A gene that turns other genes either on, making them active, or off, making them inactive.

Replication Cell cycle process of making an exact copy of the DNA so that the cell can divide, providing each new cell with a complete DNA.

Replication fork Chemical process that untwists a DNA helix allowing it to be copied for cell division.

Reporter A radioactive or other marker attached to a probe so that it can be located.

Restriction enzyme (endonuclease) Protein that homes in on a particular genetic sequence and makes a cut (dissolves the connection).

RFLP (restriction fragment length polymorphism) The portion of an individual's DNA that is unique. RFLPs are used in identification.

Ribosome Cell organelle that builds proteins.

RNA (ribonucleic acid) Chemical molecule that carries a cell's genetic instructions from the DNA to cell organelles that produce proteins for cell activities.

RNA polymerase Enzyme that straightens out a segment of DNA, allowing transcription.

Scanning tunneling microscopy Method of DNA sequencing that examines each labeled base, one atom at a time, until the label is identified.

Second messenger Chemical that sends genetic instructions after those received from messenger RNA. Second messenger instructions are for turning genes on or off.

Segregation (separation), law of Genetics rule written by Gregor Mendel stating that when plants reproduce sexually, the next generation gets half its genetic material from each parent.

Sequencing Identifying each base pair in a DNA segment.

Southern transfer Also known as Southern blot; technique for identifying RFLPs and making them visible. It is named for its developer, Dr. Edwin Southern.

Stem cell Generalized cell that can be turned into one for a specific organ.

STS (sequence tagged site) Unique identifying sequences for a gene or probe, used in making genome maps.

Superovulation Process of making a female release many eggs rather than the normal number.

Synthesis See *replication*.

Telomere End structure of a chromosome.

Theory of evolution See *evolution, theory of.*

Thymine (T) A DNA pyrimidine.

Transcription Process of copying a portion of DNA into RNA, so that a protein can be formed.

Transgenic (transplanted **gen**es) A cell or organism containing genes from another organism or species.

Translation Reading of an RNA sequence by a ribosome and producing the specified protein.

Triplet Also called a codon; series of three consecutive nucleotides that contains the instructions for a single amino acid.

Tumor suppressor gene A gene that prevents cancer as long as it is active and normal. If the gene is damaged or missing, cancer is allowed to develop.

Uracil (U) An RNA pyrimidine; counterpart of DNA's thymine (T).

Vector A carrier, such as a virus or bacteria, that carries genetically engineered DNA to another cell.

Virus A minute acellular parasite made of a nucleic acid (usually DNA) surrounded by a protein coat; it can easily enter one-celled or more complex organisms. A virus cannot live independently but must be part of a cell. Viruses that enter bacteria are called bacteriophages and are used in genetic engineering.

YAC (yeast artificial chromosome) A chromosome sequence grown in yeast cells and preserved in collections (libraries) for scientific use.

FURTHER READING

Dudley, William, editor. *Genetic Engineering: Opposing Viewpoints.* San Diego, CA: Greenhaven Press, Inc., 1990. Opinions of various experts on the subject of genetic engineering.

Judson, Horace F. *The Eighth Day of Creation.* New York: Simon and Schuster, 1979. A history of modern genetics, with emphasis on the people who made the discoveries. The book is comprehensive, but longer than most young people may want to read.

Rifkin, Jeremy. *Declaration of a Heretic.* Boston: Routledge & Kegan Paul, 1985. Point of view and philosophy of an activist who urges extreme caution in the use of genetic engineering and other new technologies.

Suzuki, David and Peter Knudtson. *Genethics: The Clash Between the New Genetics and Human Values,* revised ed. Cambridge, MA: Harvard University Press, 1990. A readable overview of evolution, plant and animal genetics, genetic engineering techniques, and the ethics of gene manipulation.

Watson, James. *The Double Helix.* New York: Atheneum, 1968. A highly personal account of the discovery of DNA's structure by one of the discoverers. This book was one of the first in which a scientist discussed the way scientists really work and interact as colleagues and rivals.

Wills, Christopher. *Exons, Introns, and Talking Genes. The Science Behind the Human Genome Project.* New York: Basic Books, 1991. A discussion of cancer, DNA, gene therapy, politics, the technology of genome sequencing, and the ethical and social considerations of this knowledge.

———. *The Wisdom of the Genes. New Pathways in Evolution.* New York: Basic Books, 1989. A series of very readable essays by a biologist who discusses evolution, mutations, and modern genetics in terms of his own life and work.

Wingerson, Lois. *Mapping Our Genes. The Genome Project and the Future of Medicine.* New York: Penguin, 1990. A description of the human genome project, emphasizing the scientists and the people who suffer from genetic diseases more than the science and technology. The author presents arguments both for and against the project.

INDEX

Italic numbers indicate illustrations.

A

acquired immune deficiency
    syndrome *See AIDS*
actin 25
ADA deficiency *See "bubble boy"*
    disease
adapter molecule *38*
adenine (A) 11, 15, 16, 18–19, 30,
    36, 61, 70, 93, 105
adenosine deaminase 81
adenosine triphosphate *See ATP*
adenovirus 52
AFP *See alpha-fetoprotein*
agriculture *See also cattle; chickens;*
    pigs; sheep
    history of 2
    patents 100
    plant research 52–56
Agriculture, U.S. Department of 55
Agrobacterium tumefaciens 52, 53
AIDS (acquired immune deficiency
    syndrome) 78
alanine 19, *38*
alpha-fetoprotein (AFP) 76–78
Alzheimer's disease 70
American Cyanamid Corporation 48
American Diabetes Association 73
American Type Culture Collection
    101
amino acids 10, 18, 19, 28, 29, 36,
    37, 48, 55, 86
amniocentesis 76
amplification 84, 105
anaphase 32, *33, 34*
anemia *See sickle-cell anemia*
animalcules 5
antigens 52
apartic acid 19
Arabidopsis thaliana 99
arginine 19
artificial insemination 41

aspartic acid *38*
ATP (adenosine triphosphate) 24,
    27, 105
AUG (mRNA codon) 36, 37
autorad (autoradiogram or
    autoradiograph) 61, 64, *98,* 105
autosomes 35, 78
Avery, Oswald 10

B

Bacillus thuringiensis 54, 56
bacteria 10, 21, 22, 43, 105
    animalcules 5
    gene therapy 80
    mitochondria 23
    prokaryotic 23
    rbST 47–48
    recombinant vaccines 51
    ribosomes 48
    transgenic animals 41
bacteriophage 86, 105
base pairs 11, 15, 23, 30, 70, 86, 92,
    105
bases 11, 105
Beadle, George Wells 11
bGH (bovine growth hormone) *See*
    bovine somatotropin
biotechnology 102–104
birth defects 73, 75–78
black tulip 2, 40
Black Tulip, The (book) 2
bladder cancer 86–87
blood disorders *See sickle-cell*
    anemia; thalassemia
bovine growth hormone *See bovine*
    somatotropin
bovine somatotropin (bST) 46–51
breast cancer cell *83*
"bubble boy" disease 81

INDEX

C

Caenorhabditis elegans 98
camels 2
cancer 83–91
cap (nucleotide sequence) 36
carbon atom 13
cattle See also transgenic animals
   bovine growth hormone 46–51
   breeding of 2, 40–41
   Marfan syndrome 69
   vaccines 51–52
cdc genes (cell-division genes) 27
cDNA See complementary DNA
cell 1, 6, 7, 10, 17, 21–39, 105
cell cortex 25
cell cultures 40
cell cycle 20, 25–28, 26, 35, 73, 83, 84, 105
cell differentiation 25–26, 105
cell-division genes See cdc genes
cell membrane (cell wall) 25, 105
cell science 4, 8
cell splitting See meiosis; mitosis
centimorgan (cM) 95, 105
Chargaff, Erwin 14
Chase, Martha 10
chickens 42
chorionic villus sampling 76
chromatin 22, 105
chromosomes 1, 7, 8, 18, 23, 30, 35, 37, 106
   chromosome 4 93
   chromosome 5 86
   chromosome 6 74
   chromosome 7 71, 93
   chromosome 11 74, 75, 80, 93
   chromosome 13 85
   chromosome 15 67–68
   chromosome 16 76
   chromosome 17 86
   chromosome 19 75
   chromosome 20 75
   chromosome 21 76, 77, 94
   replication of 31
   X chromosome See X chromosome
   Y chromosome See Y chromosome
cleavage 35
cleaving 60
clock theory 26–27
cloning 42, 106
cM See centimorgan
codons (triplets) 18, 37, 106
Collins, Francis 71

complementary DNA (cDNA) 101–102, 106
complex cells See eukaryotes
Consumers Union 49–50
contigs 96
corn 2, 102
Crick, Francis 11, 14–15, 17
criminal investigation See DNA fingerprinting
Crittenden, Lyman 42
crops See agriculture
crossing over 9, 106
cyclins 27–28, 106
cysteine 19
cystic fibrosis 70–72, 81
cytokinesis 32, 33
cytoplasm 23, 25, 28, 29, 36, 37, 106
cytosine (C) 11, 15, 16, 18–19, 31, 36, 37, 61, 93, 106
cytoskeleton 23, 106

D

Darwin, Charles 7, 8
Defense, U.S. Department of 57
deletion 52, 70, 106
deoxyribonucleic acid See DNA
deoxyribose 16
diabetes 73–75, 82
differentiation See cell differentiation
diseases See names of specific diseases
DNA (deoxyribonucleic acid) 17, 17–18, 21, 106
   cloned molecules 96
   components 13
   copying process 30–31
   discovery of 10–18
   G_1 phase 25, 26, 28
   genetic code 18–19
   human genome project 92–98, 94–95
   kinases 27
   Marfan syndrome 68
   mitochondria 23
   patenting of 101–102
   restriction fragment length polymorphisms (RFLPs) 57–59
   segment deletion/insertion 58
   sequencing system 60
   S phase 30–31
   structure of 12–16, 16

transgenic animals 42
DNA fingerprinting (DNA typing)
57–59, 63–66, 96, 106
DNA ligase 43, 106
DNA tissue typing 74
dogs 2
dominance, law of 3, 8, 106
dominant traits 3–4
domino theory 26–27
double helix 10, 14, *15*, 17–18, 106
Down syndrome 75–78, *77*
Drosophila melanogaster 9, 93, 99
Duchenne muscular dystrophy 81
Dumas, Alexandre 2
dystrophin 81

E

E. coli 51, 76, 98–99
egg 25, 32
electrophoresis 60, 64–65, 97
Ellstrand, Norman 56
embryo 32
endoplasmic reticulum 24, 106
Energy, U.S. Department of 93
epilepsy 70
Escherichia coli See E. coli
ethics 68, 72
euchromatin 22, 106
eugenics movement 79–80
eukaryotes 22, 23, 30, 106
evolution, theory of 7–8, 106
exclusion 63
exons 36, 107
extracellular matrix 25
eye color 1, 9

F

family traits *See inheritance traits*
Federal Bureau of Investigation (FBI)
63
fertilization 25, 32
Flint, Hollis *54*
flow cytometry 98, 107
Food and Drug Administration
(FDA) 48, 50
"fragile X" syndrome 75–76
Franklin, Rosalind 11
Fraumeni, Joseph 87, *88*

G

G0 phase 25, *26*, 35
G1 phase 25–30
G2 phase 25, *26*, 31–35
Galletta, Gene *55*
gametes 25
gel electrophoresis 97
gene, definition of 1, 107
gene amplification *See* amplification
gene carrier 72
gene splicing 43, 107
gene therapy 79–82
    for cancer 89–90
genetic code 18, *19*, 107
genetic defects 30, 69–70
genetic engineering
    beginnings of 18
    definition of 107
genetic fingerprinting *See DNA
    fingerprinting*
genetic maps *See linkage maps,
    physical maps, genome mapping*
genetics, foundation of 2–4
genetic susceptibility 73, 107
genome 92, 107
genome mapping 92–97, 104, 107
glucose 73
glutamic acid 19
glutamine 19
glycine 19
glycogen 73
Goldstein, Joseph L. 104
Golgi bodies 24, 107
growth factors 28, 29, 86, 107
guanine (G) 11, *15*, 16, 18–19, 31,
    36, 37, 61, 70, 93, 107

H

hair color 1
Hammerschlag, Freddi *53*
Harvard mouse 100–101
helix 11, 35, 107
hemophilia 78–79
hereditary unit *See gene, definition of*
herpes 52
Hershey, Alfred 10
heterochromatin 22, 107
heterozygote (hybrid) 4, 107
histidine 19
histone 30
HLA (human leukocyte antigen) 74
homeobox 99, 107

homozygote 3, 107
homunculus 5
Hooke, Robert 5
horses 2
Human Genome Organization 93
human genome project 92–98
human leukocyte antigen *See HLA*
hybrid (heterozygote) 4, 107
hybridization 61, *62*, 98, 108
hybridoma 103, 108
hydrogen atom 13

I

identification 56
IGF-1 *See insulinlike growth factor-1*
immortal cell 80, 108
immune system B lymphocyte 103
inclusion 63
independent assortment, law of 4, 9, 108
inheritance, laws of 2–4, 58
insertion 58, 108
insulin 73
insulinlike growth factor-1 (IGF-1) 49–50
intermediary filaments 23, 108
introns 36, 43, 108
in vitro fertilization 45, 72
ion channels 25
islets of Langerhans 73–75
isoleucine 19
isotopes 61, 108

J

Jacob, Francois 18
Jeffreys, Alec 63

K

kinases 27, 29, 108

L

Lee, Wen-Hwa 85
Leeuwenhoek, Antonius van 5, *6*
leucine 18, 19
Li, Frederick 87, *88*
Li-Fraumeni syndrome 87–88
Lilly and Company, Eli 48
lima beans *54*

Lincoln, Abraham 67–68
linkage 9, 108
linkage maps 9, 43, 95, 108
livestock *See cattle*; *chickens*; *pigs*; *sheep*
loci 58, 108
lysosomes 24, 108

M

macrorestriction map 96, 108
Marfan syndrome 67–69
Margulis, Lynn 21
Mass, John *55*
mastitis 41, 50
Matthei, Heinrich 18
maturation 36
maturity-onset diabetes of the young (MODY) 73
M.C.C. (tumor suppressor gene) 86
meiosis 25, 27, 32, *34*, 35, 95, 108
melanoma therapy 90–91
Mendel, Gregor 2–4, *3*, 6, 8, 9, 58
Mendelian inheritance 2–4, 108
mental retardation 75–78, 79
messenger RNA (mRNA) 29, 36, 37, *38*, 102, 108
metaphase 32, *33*, *34*
methionine 19, 36, 37
mice 99
    genetically engineered 100
    transgenic animals 44
microfilaments 23, 108
microscope 4–5, *5*
microtubules 23, 109
milk 47–51
Mirsky, Arthur 10
missense mutations 86, 109
mitochondria 23, *24*, 32, 70, 99, 104, 109
mitochondrial DNA (mtDNA) 23, 70, 109
mitochondrial inheritance 70
mitosis (M phase) 25, *26*, 27, 32, *33*, 109
MODY (maturity-onset diabetes of the young) 73
molecular biology 17, 109
monoclonal antibodies 40, 103, 104, 109
Monod, Jacques 18
Monsanto Chemical Company 48
Morgan, Thomas Hunt 9, 95

M phase *See mitosis*
mRNA *See messenger RNA*
mtDNA *see mitochondrial DNA*
multifactorial changes 70, 109
multiple foci 73
muscular dystrophy 81
mutations 10, 109
myc (oncogene) 85
Mycoplasma capricolum 98
myeloma cells 103
myoblasts 81

N

National Farmers Union 49
National Institutes of Health (NIH)
 50, 80, 93
nematode (roundworm) 98
neural tube defects 76
Nirenberg, Marshall 18
nitrogen 13, 55
non-Mendelian inheritance 109
nonsense mutations 86, 109
nuclear DNA 70
nuclear matrix 23, 109
nuclear membrane 23
nuclear transplantation 44, *45*, 109
nucleic acid 10, 17, 40
nucleoli 23, 109
nucleotides 10, 30, 36, 37, 109
 base change 58
 chain of *12*
 structure of *11*
nucleus *7, 22*, 22–23, 29, 109

O

oligonucleotides 74, 109
oncogenes *84*, 85, 86, 109
oocyte 35
ordered clone map 96, 109
organelles 23, 24, 109
ovulation 35
oxygen atom 13

P

p53 gene 86, 87–88
Pardee, Arthur 28
Pasteur, Louis 6, *7*
pastoralism 40–41
patents 99–100

crops 100
DNA materials 101–102
genetically engineered organisms
 100–101
Pauling, Linus 11, *14*
PCR *See polymerase chain reaction*
peas 2–4, 6, 40
pesticides *54*, 55–56
petunias 40, 52
phenylalanine 19
phosphatase enzymes 28
phosphates 13, 16, 27
phosphoric acid 11
phosphorus 13
phosphorus-32 61
photosynthesis 24, 55
physical maps 95–96, 110
pigs 51
plants 2
 research projects 52–56
plasma membrane 25
plasmids 43, 110
plastids 24, 110
point mutation 70, 110
polar body 35
pollen 55
poly A sequence 36
polymerase chain reaction (PCR) 40,
 86, 97, 109
polymers 25
polymorphisms 58, 110
primers 97, 110
probe binding 60–63, 110
prokaryotes 22, 30, 110
proline 19
prophase 32, *33, 34*
proteins 10, 17, 25
protein synthesis *38*
protoplasm 7
Provencher, Leonard *42*
pseudorabies 52
purines 11, 14, 15, 18, 110
Pursel, Vernon *47*
pyrimidines 11, 14, 15, 17, 18, 110

Q

quiescent phase (G_0) 25, *26,* 35

R

rabies 52
Rasputin 78

rbST *See recombinant somatropin*
receptors 25, 29, 86, 110
recessive trait 3–4
recognition sites 58, 110
recombinant DNA 40, 110
Recombinant DNA Advisory
   Committee of the National
   Institutes of Health 80
recombinant plasmid 43
recombinant somatotropin (rbST)
   47–51
recombinant vaccines 51–52
regulator genes 18, 110
replication (synthesis) 25, 30–31, 110
replication fork 30, *31*, 110
reporter 61, 110
restriction enzymes 43, 60, 110
retinoblastoma *85*
reverse transcription 102
RFLPs (restriction fragment length
   polymorphisms) 58, *59*, 60, 96, 110
ribonucleic acid *See RNA*
ribosomes 24, 29, 36, *38*, 110
rice 2, 53, 102
Rifkin, Jeremy 49
rinderpest 52
Riordan, Jack 71
RNA (ribonucleic acid) 10, 11,
   17–18, 110
   G₁ phase 28–30
   maturation 36
   mitochondria 23
   nucleoli 23
   quiescent phase 35
   S phase 36
   transgenic animals 42
   translation 36–37
RNA polymerase 36, 111
roundworm *See nematode*

S

Saccharomyces cerevisiae 98
salmonella 51
scanning tunneling microscopy 98,
   111
second messengers 29, 111
segregation (separation), law of 2, 8,
   111
selective breeding 41
sequence tagged site (STS) 96–97,
   111
sequencing 71, 97–98, 111

serine 19, *38*
sexual reproduction 1
   chromosomes and 8–10
   in plants 2, 6
sheep 2
sickle-cell anemia 80
smallpox 51
somatic cell therapy 80
somatotropin 46
Southern, Edwin 60
Southern transfer 60, 111
soybeans 55
sperm 25, 32, 41
spermatocyte 32
S phase 25, *26*, 27, 30, 35, 73
spindle forms 32
spontaneous generation 7
stem cells 25, 44, 80, 111
stomatitis 51
STS *See sequence tagged site*
sugar molecules 11, 13
superovulation 43–44, 111
syndromes *See AIDS; Down
   syndrome; "fragile X" syndrome;
   Li-Fraumeni syndrome; Marfan
   syndrome*
synthesis *See replication*

T

taxol 103
T cells 81
technology transfer 102, 103
telomere 31, 111
telophase 32, *33, 34*
thalassemia 80
Theologis, Athanasios *61*
threonine 19
thymine (T) 11, 16, 17, 18–19, 31,
   36, 61, 93, 111
TILs *See tumor infiltrating
   lymphocytes*
tissues 21
tomatoes 53, 102
toxic substances 37
transcription 36, 111
transgenic, definition of 41, 111
transgenic animals 41–46, 104
translation 36–37, 37, 111
triplets (codons) 18, 37, 111
tRNA (transfer RNA) 37
tryptophan 19
Tsui, Lap-Chee *71*

tulip-growing 2
tumor infiltrating lymphocytes
(TILs) 90
tumor necrosis factor 90
tumor suppressors 85–86, 111
typing *See DNA fingerprinting*
tyrosine 19

U

ultraviolet radiation 37
Upjohn Corporation 48
uracil (U) 17, 111

V

vaccines 51–52
valine 19, *38*
vectors 43, 44, 89, 111
vesicular stomatitis 51
Victoria (British queen) 78

viruses 10, 41, 80, 111
Vogelstein, Bert 86, *87*

W

Watson, James 11, 14–15, 93
wheat 2
Wilkins, Maurice 11

X

X chromosome 8–10, 32, 35, 67, 75,
77, 78–79, 81, 93

Y

YACs (yeast artificial chromosomes)
76, 96, 112
Y chromosome 8–10, 32, 35, 67